23 Goals + Objectives
35 Stewards vs. Served ?

W9-APS-022

Structure Your Church for Mission

Kurt Bickel and Les Stroh
©2010

STRUCTURE YOUR CHURCH FOR MISSION
Strobickan Publishing LLC, Orlando, Florida

Copyright © 2010 Kurt Bickel and Les Stroh. All rights reserved.

ISBN 978-0-9798057-2-1

Printed in the United States of America, E. O. Painter Printing Company, DeLeon Springs, FL

Scripture quotations are from the NRSV © 1989 by the division of Christian Education of the National Council of the Churches of Christ in the USA. Used by permission. All rights reserved.

This book may not be reproduced in whole or in part by any means whatsoever without written permission from:

Strobickan Publishing LLC
3811 Laguna Street
Orlando Florida, 32805

Layout and cover design by John Rallison, Thambos Media Works (www.thambos.net)

The Aligned Missional Structure is based upon the Cornerstone Factor which was developed by Kurt Bickel, Daryl Pichan and Les Stroh. © 2001 all rights reserved.

www.CornerstoneFactor.com

This book is dedicated to our
consulting partner

Daryl Pichan

who brings clarity, connection and
courage to our team.

CONTENTS

ALIGNMENT

Prologue

For the Sake of the Mission

*'Rejoice with me, for I have
found the coin that I had lost.'
Just so, I tell you, there is joy in
the presence of the angels of God
over one sinner who repents.*

Luke 15:9-10 (NRSV)

Structuring your congregation for mission would be important even if it is only from an organizational and behavioral perspective. All systems periodically need the renewal of a good planning process. However, we are hoping that is not why you acquired this book. We imagine you share our passion for building the kingdom of God. You find it an incredible joy and privilege to be a steward of Christ's ministry. Your baptism inspires you to daily repentance and daily commitment to take up the cross of Jesus Christ. The humbling idea of being a leader for the sake of the Gospel keeps you striving with conviction to advance the mission.

Structuring your congregation for mission would be important even if it is only to revive a church that is experiencing decline and suffering losses. All systems periodically need to increase their efforts to sustain the organization. However, we envision that you seek so much more than a better congregation. You long for a fellowship of believers that, by the power of the Spirit, can overcome the principalities and powers of this world and firmly establish a spirit of hope, peace and grace that will indeed transform your whole community.

Structuring your congregation for mission would be important even if it is only to increase the commitment of your membership to the congregation. All systems need to have the support and cooperation of their membership in order to grow, yet we believe that you desire more than people committed to an institution. You fervently pray for a congregation deeply convicted and fully mobilized for service in the kingdom of God.

Structuring your congregation for mission would be important even if it is only to improve stewardship in the lives of leaders and members. All systems need the investment of time and dollars to sustain both agency and program. Still, we are certain that you would rather have partners in the Gospel who love the Lord with all their hearts, with their entire minds and with all their souls. You desire women and men who are passionate about being disciples in every single aspect of their lives.

Structuring your congregation for mission would be important even if it is only to better serve your members. All systems benefit from better customer service. Nevertheless, we suspect that you are yearning for a church that selflessly ministers to the helpless, the hopeless and the hurting. You pray for a congregation that would be the body of Christ in the community, offering unconditional love and compassion for all who are lost and abandoned. You desire people whose witness is congruent in word and action. You rejoice over each one who comes just a little closer to the truth in Jesus. When a lost person is restored to the heavenly Father, you join with all of heaven to celebrate with inexplicable joy.

We pray that your faith, passion, awareness, dedication and understanding will lead to heroic and effective leadership in the kingdom of God. Structuring your congregation for mission is tedious work, demanding diligent coordination and management; yet you will not do it merely for the sake of leadership. You are a steward for the sake of the mission. You are a steward leader for the sake of Jesus.

Chapter 1

Structure
Matters

We are the church together.

Yes, as the children's song says, "we are the church" and God has a plan for His church. He continues to unfold this plan with the assurance that the victory is already won in Christ's birth, death and resurrection. God's strategy for saving people is so marvelous it defies human comprehension. God determined that the church, a royal priesthood of people, would continue the mission of proclaiming Christ's victory to the ends of the earth until the end of time. His missional plan for the church is perfect.

Throughout the centuries, despite hatred, persecution and bombardment from evil forces against it, the holy church has survived. Throughout the centuries, despite false doctrine, corruption and evil forces from within, the holy and invisible bride of Christ has thrived. While God's plan is perfect, the organization He has chosen to implement the plan is not. Even though its mission mandate is clear, the church struggles. Why is it that congregations so often end up with less than they had hoped for? Why do congregations have trouble supporting their members as Spirit-led stewards living out the mission as the Body of Christ in the world? There is an old saying, "Organizations are perfectly structured to get the results they get." We believe if congregations want to get more – more witness, more discipleship, more worship and more missions – they should examine how they are structured.

Together we share over thirty years of experience serving congregations who want to get more. These congregations know God's grace is immeasurable, yet they are praying, preparing and planning for measurable growth. We have had the privilege of facilitating consultations of prayer and preparation that foster positive changes that close the gap between God's vision and the congregation's action. In all of this, we have learned that structure matters.

We have repeatedly encountered the problem of inadequate organization, ambiguous responsibilities, poor preparation and diffused efforts. It is not a lack of faithfulness; it is a lack of insight and role clarity. Moses was bogged down serving as judge for the children of Israel until his father-in-law suggested a structural change. Moses appointed "officials over thousands, hundreds, fifties and tens" (Exodus 18:21 NRSV). These officials would be judges for the people. Moses demonstrated insight and clarity for his role. He changed the structure. It was not change for the sake of change. Moses was still able to be the people's representative to God. Effective structure is not the mission; it is the tool for achieving the mission.

In this book we introduce a few theories about organizational development. Initially, we discuss the essential alignment of capacity and competency for congregational life and mission. In Chapter 3 we consider the alignment of governance and operations within the church structure. In Chapter 4 we initiate the discussion of a model for a missional congregation. It is the active alignment of governance and operations that supports Spirit-led stewards living as the Body of Christ in the world. We share our observations regarding misaligned structures and the poor communication, conflict, ambiguity and frustration that happen as a result. In Chapter 5 we talk about the people in congregations and look at the various roles of leadership and management. We compare two predominate church governance structures in Chapter 6 and underscore the strengths and weaknesses of each. Chapter 7 is our affirmation of aligned governance and operations for effective missional churches. Chapter 8 is about the operation effort of the congregation. Chapter 9 details the implementation of the model. Chapter 10 provides an outline for the development of a governance manual.

This book is not only about organizational charts and models. It is about people. God likes people. He wants people to be the church – people who by grace are doing together what they cannot do alone. His plan is to have more people in the church. Chairpersons, presidents, clergy, teachers, missionaries, deacons, ministers, ushers and elders are all baptized people of God. The assembly, the voters, the congregation and the members are all baptized people of God. The Church Council, the Vestry and the Board of Directors are all baptized people of God. "But you are a chosen race, a royal priesthood, a holy nation, God's own people, in order that you may proclaim the mighty acts of him who called you out of darkness into his marvelous light. Once you were not a people, but now you are God's people; once you had not received mercy, but now you have received mercy" (1 Peter 2:9-10 NRSV). An essential ingredient of congregational structure is the definition of the roles and responsibilities of people.

Church doctrine is important when considering church structure. Weak or ill-defined structure does not necessarily mean weak or ill-defined theology. However, structure that is disconnected from doctrine can have a neutral or even negative effect upon the mission. This is not a theological study of church structure. We will depend upon your congregation and the Holy Spirit to determine how our recommendations on structure are aligned with your doctrine and foundational principles. Our expertise is in the area of organizational development and leadership. We will, however, not pretend that applied behavioral science is the only remedy for sluggish congregations. We are deeply committed to the power of the Gospel for the transformation of leaders and their organizations. We pray that you will be engaged in a process that will inspire greater personal commitment to excellence and a passion for our Savior's mission.

*Finally, beloved, whatever
is true, whatever is noble,
whatever is right, whatever
is pure, whatever is lovely,
whatever is admirable – if
anything is excellent or
praiseworthy – think about
such things.*

Philippians 4:8 (NRSV)

Chapter 2
Alignment

*Laws are like sausages. It's better
not to see them being made.*

Otto von Bismarck

CONGREGATIONAL LIFE

Congregational life is complex. At times, it is even chaotic. Attempting to organize the church may feel like sweeping up marbles. Because the church is comprised of sinful people, there are many problems; some are just annoying while others are painfully destructive. Even though models are both a simplification and an exaggeration of reality, we will use a model to describe, simplify and ultimately organize our thinking about the unpredictable congregation. It is a *being/doing* model.

Think of all aspects of congregational life and divide them in two directions. Put all of what the congregation IS on the vertical *being* axis, and put all the things that the congregation DOES on the horizontal *doing* axis. This fundamental distinction helps define the alignment of the earthly *doing* of the church with the incarnation of Christ in the *being* of the church. The *being* of the church has a transcendent quality. The *doing* of the church is the human transitory response. Both are essential to mission.

ALIGNMENT

There is a tendency on the part of congregations to place too much emphasis on one axis or the other. Some churches live exclusively on the side of who they are *being*. "We are the called, redeemed people of God. That is what is important. That is all that really matters." This sounds New Testament familiar: "They answered him, 'We are descendants of Abraham and have never been slaves to anyone'" (John 8:33 NRSV).

In contrast, a congregation may spend too much time on the axis of *doing*. Its people celebrate how busy they are and how many ministries they have going, yet somehow fail to sustain effective and significant mission work. There may be many ministry trans-actions, but people are not being transformed. A congregation can get so wrapped up in taking care of those who are already in the faith that they neglect the work of the Spirit in the lives of unbelievers. Busyness is not necessarily a sign of faithfulness, and neither is purity of doctrine.

The challenge of the *being/doing* model is maintaining balance.

Life is a balancing process. Faithfulness is a balancing process. This balance or dynamic alignment is not fixed or frozen. Individuals, families or congregations are never held in perfect balance. The doctrine of law and grace provides a competing tension and this tension is not reconciled by one having dominance over the other. The believer balances the law that condemns and the grace that liberates. The whole of creation groans because it is out of alignment with God's perfect design (Romans 8). That is what we recognize as alignment with *being* and *doing*. The synthesis of these different and often opposing forces is of great value to the structure of a congregation.

A misaligned congregation is either too busy to remember why the church exists or too focused on the mystery and majesty of the church to make practical applications. Church leaders who get trapped in a "one-or-the-other" approach to what they perceive to be competing issues end up in a "lose-lose" situation. Their congregation either focuses on the ethos and ritual or leans heavily on busy activity. Responding to issues in this way will simply push the congregation further out of alignment. A healthy productive congregation is led by people who understand the absolute necessity of aligning the *being* and the *doing* of the church within their own congregation.

THE ALIGNED CORNERSTONE

In the year 1160, Maurice de Sully proclaimed the vision of a grand cathedral to be constructed in Paris. Three years later, he stood on the island in the Seine River where the Celts had held their services, and where, atop their sacred groves, the Romans had built their own temple to Jupiter. There he placed the cornerstone of the future and not yet visible Notre Dame de Paris. When he died in 1196, only the nave had been completed. The structure was not finished until 1250. The entire cathedral was built upon the vision of de Sully and the cornerstone he had put in place. The cornerstone was more than a block of stone; it was also the symbol of the hopes and aspirations of the people. The careful placement of the cornerstone and the alignment of each successive stone that followed for nearly a century of construction erected a building. The determination of the generations of people produced the cathedral "Our Lady." It has stood throughout the centuries because of an alignment of vision and stones. Missional direction will also benefit from such alignment of vision and action. Just as the grand cathedral was built upon what was envisioned and the work it took to get the job done, the mission of the congregation is accomplished when its *being* and *doing* are properly aligned.

*For just as the body without the
spirit is dead, so faith without
works is also dead.*

James 2:26 (NRSV)

Chapter 3

Nothing Good Comes from Confusion

That which comes after, ever conforms
to that which has gone before.

Marcus Aurelius

We have conducted many interviews with congregational leaders and have repeatedly heard, "What our church really needs is a vision!" We have discovered the real problem, however, is not the lack of a vision, but too many visions. Each person seems to have a different view of what the church should do, with little understanding of what the church should be.

Church leaders must, through prayer and preparation, arrive at a common vision – an understanding of what God would have the congregation be in the world. Confusion also arises because so much of what the church does is positive and even God-pleasing, yet not effective for the sake of the mission.

Confusion in the congregation is caused by the lack of clarity between *being* and *doing*. It is also caused by fuzzy role definition and ambiguous priorities. Nothing good comes from confusion. It is the responsibility of the leadership to create priorities and establish clear roles.

Exercise

While the church is not a business, we can further our discussion of organizational structure in congregations by asking a few "business type" questions.

Think about your congregation in business terms. How would you respond to these questions? Ask your congregation's leaders to answer all the questions and then compare your responses.

1. Who are the owners?
2. Who are the customers?
3. Who are the employees?
4. Who is the boss, CEO, president?
5. Who is the Board of Directors?
6. Who is the chief financial officer?
7. Who is the chief operations officer?
8. To whom do employees go with suggestions for new products or services?
9. How do employees know whether their work is satisfactory?
10. Who determines what gets funded?

The dialog that follows this exercise can be revealing. Congregational leaders, many who have a good understanding of business, give a wide assortment of answers. Difficulties arise from having "different" answers. Different answers reveal ambiguity. Misunderstanding regarding the structure of the congregation leads to poor communication, faulty cooperation, overwork and burn-out. Differing expectations lead to unmet expectations, and unmet expectations lead to conflict. If you are experiencing any of these challenges, the solution may be found in an organizational structure that properly aligns the governance and the operations in your congregation.

One of our client congregations was experiencing significant tension and anxiety because the Senior Pastor and Board of Deacons were deeply conflicted over several issues within the congregation. They were at odds about the process for reclaiming delinquent members; they disagreed about the strategies for the spiritual care of the members. This was indeed the presenting issue needing attention, however, we soon discovered the deeper problem came from the way both the Deacons and the Pastor understood their authority and responsibility toward each other. While the congregational by-laws established the roles of both Pastor and Deacons, they were silent regarding how the Pastor and Deacons were to interact. The Pastor and Deacons could not determine how to serve the members until they determined the specific authority and responsibilities toward one another. When they decided upon a workable and God-pleasing structure, they were able to resolve their conflict and engage in mission.

GOVERNANCE AND OPERATIONS

The two basic functions in any congregation are governance and operations. The first step in establishing an effective congregational structure is to ascribe every aspect of the congregation to the governance – *being* or the operations – *doing* of the church. This basic delineation helps clarify a vision and focus the actions. Differentiating between governance and operations will empower you to manage complexity and be decisive in spite of ambiguity.

Governance is focused on right *being*. Operations are focused on right *doing*. Look at the ten items below under both governance and operations.

GOVERNANCE

1. Determining ends (what)
2. Developing and selecting leaders
3. Articulating Core Values, Mission, Vision, Critical Targets and Goals
4. Being proactive

5. Looking at the big picture
6. Staying focused on what is strategic
7. Defining long-range priorities
8. Delegating responsibility and authority
9. Establishing governance policies
10. Monitoring the whole

OPERATIONS

1. Determining means (how)
2. Empowering managers
3. Setting Objectives and Action Plans
4. Reacting to Strategic Direction
5. Giving attention to details
6. Focusing on the short range
7. Designing immediate plans
8. Staying accountable to delegated responsibility
9. Establishing and carrying out procedure
10. Managing the parts

Which structural dynamic gets most of the attention, time and energy in your congregation? Is it governance or operations? How much meeting time is spent on each dynamic?

A congregation once asked us to facilitate their annual Board retreat. The phone conversation between the Consultant and the Pastor went something like this:

Consultant: What will be the goal of the retreat?
Pastor: We will be working on a vision for our congregation.
C: Do you currently have a vision?
P: Yes, we developed one last year.
C: So how is last year's vision development working for you?
P: Well, that's just it. We feel we haven't really done much about it, and we need to get back at it and advance to the next steps.

C: Why do you think you haven't been able to work toward the vision since the last retreat?

P: We have been so busy with hiring a new Associate Pastor and working on our sagging stewardship.

C: How will this year be different because of the retreat?

P: The retreat is a chance to talk and pray together about the future of our church. We hope to restore our enthusiasm for the vision and come back pumped up. But with volunteer leadership, it is hard to sustain the energy.

C: What would happen if you spent this retreat considering why your structure keeps you from implementing your vision?

P: Well, we don't want to spend time on by-laws and constitution when the mission needs work.

This congregation is having difficulty sustaining an effective pursuit of its mission because it fails to divide the work between the means and the ends. Governance is more about prayer, Bible study, dialog, preparation and thinking. Operations is more about coordinating, implementing and evaluating. Perhaps the same people can work on governance and operations but not at the same time. The failure to separate these two dynamics will frustrate and confuse the system.

When you have distinctive alignment between governance and operations, you will be better able to remove the confusion that hinders the pursuit of your mission of proclaiming Christ's victory to the ends of the earth until the end of time.

All things should be done decently and in order.

1 Corinthians 14:40 (NRSV)

Chapter 4
The Missional Structure

Progress occurs when courageous,
skillful leaders seize the opportunity
to change things for the better.

Harry S. Truman

A JIGSAW PUZZLE

A helpful metaphor for this chapter comes from seeing Joe's jigsaw puzzle table. Joe loved to put together puzzles. The more elaborate the better. Joe built a special table for his jigsaw puzzle assembly area. Flat boxes were taped all around the edges of the table. Each box represented a different type of puzzle piece. There was a handy reference puzzle piece pattern glued to the front of each box. Before Joe put even one puzzle piece in place, he sorted all the puzzle pieces into the boxes. Corner pieces, edge pieces, double sided gaps, single sided dimples-every piece was categorized and pre-sorted. Joe knew that he would still need to correctly match color, line and shade; however, the pattern of the puzzle helped to narrow his search. When there are "structural boxes" in the church, the organizational puzzle of the congregation comes together with delightful God-given complexity, full of color in a three-dimensional world.

A dynamic, effective congregational structure supports Spirit-led stewards living their mission as the body of Christ in the world. We see a great opportunity for congregations who align their structure for vibrant mission by giving significant attention to both governance and operations. The model below is simple, yet the implementation can be challenging.

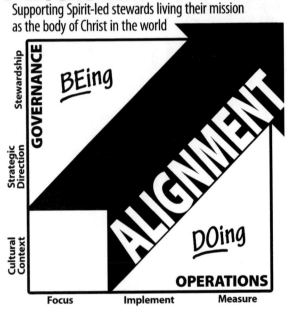

GOVERNANCE

Congregational leadership must establish a culture of governance. This includes a comprehensive awareness of the Cultural Context of the congregation, a determination of the Strategic Direction and an atmosphere of expansive and maturing Stewardship.

Cultural Context

Determining the right things for the missional efforts of the congregation begins with an awareness of the Cultural Context in which the congregation exists. This encompasses the history of the congregation, including the formation, transitions and unique stories of God's blessings over time. Cultural Context also includes the community with the current makeup of people, industry and other demographical information. The understanding of the context must include the strengths and weaknesses of the internal environment of the congregation, as well as the opportunities and threats it faces from its external environment now and into the future.

Strategic Direction

Governance must discover and focus on a Strategic Direction for the congregation. That Strategic Direction should include the following:

- The congregation's Core Values
- A Mission Statement that describes the reason for the existence of the congregation
- A Vision is a God-given description of the future in the hearts and minds of the leaders that will not fade away
- A few Critical Targets which describe either areas of effort or groups of people on which a congregation must make a significant impact
- One Corporate Goal that describes the preferred future condition for each Critical Target

The above items are an aligned, interdependent set of governance articles. These must not only be established but must be actively and passionately addressed. A congregation must harmonize its efforts to honor the Core Values, pursue the Mission, live the Vision, focus on Targets and accomplish the Goals.

Stewardship

The expansion of Christian Stewardship is the primary intent of congregational governance, not only for the congregation as a whole but for individual members as well. With an understanding of the culture into which they have been called and with a clear articulation of what the congregation intends to be for the sake of the kingdom, congregational leadership is better positioned to assist its members in answering the summons to be Spirit-led stewards in support of Christ's mission to the world. The primary model for this growth is the example of current leadership. When leadership is working with healthy, principled, Christ-centered governance, Spirit-led stewardship of others can emerge and flourish.

OPERATIONS

The developmental sequence of operations in a congregation are Focus, Implement and Measure. These three components complement the Cultural Context, Strategic Direction and Stewardship of governance; they empower an effective congregational structure to support Spirit-led stewards living their mission as the body of Christ in the world.

Focus

Those given the responsibility must clarify the operational Focus of the congregation's ministry efforts. The Strategic Direction, developed by the Governance Board, provides a broad definition of the preferred future. Under the direction of the Senior Pastor, the staff and staff volunteers put the mission into operations that develop Purpose, Goals, Objectives and Action Plans. They do this utilizing the following process:

- Each unit (an individual or group to whom a particular area of ministry has been assigned) should develop and publish a Purpose Statement. A Purpose Statement is a clear, concise statement (25 words or less) explaining why a particular unit exists and functions within the congregation.

- Each unit should articulate a set of Unit Goals. In most instances, there should be no more that five or six such goals. A Unit Goal is a description of a preferred, future condition with regard to an effective pursuit of the unit's purpose and the congregation's Strategic Direction.

- Each unit writes an Objective(s) for each goal. An Objective is a statement of specific, measurable conditions to be achieved by a designated time which contributes to the accomplishment of a Unit Goal.

- Having completed the Purpose, Goals and Objectives, the unit writes Action Plans. An Action Plan is a sequence of activities undertaken by assigned individuals within a given period of time in order to achieve an Objective.

These planning steps are critical to the life of the congregation. Too often this process is underutilized. When all units are actively planning and publishing their plans, the congregation has better prepared itself by raising up a greater awareness of the mission. Measurable objectives and timelines give a sense of accountability and responsible stewardship. It takes time, effort and coordination to publish the plan; however, the results make it worthwhile.

Implement

Without a commitment to Implement, planning is just another three-ring binder for the shelf. Implementation means the congregation is more like a three-ring circus with intentional, simultaneous activity orchestrated for mission. It is a sad reality that many congregations establish a new Strategic Direction and design the requisite Operational Path and then go about business as usual, spending their resources as they always have. An effective Operational Path requires intentional, effective implementation. That implementation means every operational transaction, including answering the phone, greeting people in the hallways and preparing and serving coffee, is an operational moment of truth. Every sermon, every Sunday school class, every hospital visit must be a reflection of the congregation aligning its day-to-day operational activities with its mission.

Measure

If you have set the proper operational unit Goals and Objectives, you have established the means by which your operational efforts can be measured to determine if they are indeed working to bring to life the Strategic Direction set by the governance Board. The ongoing assessment of "how you measure up" is an essential part of efficient stewardship. We often hear, "You can't measure spiritual growth." In some ways that is true, but you can certainly observe behaviors that indicate spiritual growth. We are not suggesting you simply ask how many events you offer or even how many people are being trained. You should be consistently asking, "What is being achieved by the ministries we are *doing*?" We believe you must pay attention to measurements and evaluations that give you current indications of progress. Are there new people in worship? Are people who were less than regular increasing their involvement in the congregation? How many more people are engaging in mission efforts, local, national or international? How many more adult baptisms were there in the last twelve months? We have heard the cry, "We are not called to be successful. We are called to be faithful." If God's people are truly *being* faithful to their calling, if they are seeking effective ways to connect people to Jesus, is it possible the Lord will not bless those efforts? We believe that the Lord will bless the efforts of faithful stewards. He will give even greater opportunities for mission to those who use their talents rather than bury them.

> **The Rev. Dr. Charles Mueller asks the right question: "So what does successless faithfulness look like?"**

People become uncomfortable about the idea of keeping track of the mission numbers such as baptisms, adult converts and increased worship attendance. If numbers aren't important, why do we know the number of the miraculous catch of fish? Why do we know how many people were fed with two fish and five barley loaves? Why do we know that the steward who returned ten talents after being given five was honored by his master? Why do we know how many were saved on Pentecost? The answer is because measurements matter, and the best measurements are about results, not activity.

> Simon Peter said to them, "I am going fishing." They said to him, "We will go with you." They went out and got into the boat, but that night they caught nothing. Just after daybreak, Jesus stood on the beach; but the disciples did not know that it was Jesus. Jesus said to them, "Children, you have no fish, have you?" They answered him, "No." He said to them, "Cast the net to the right side of the boat, and you will find some." So they cast it, and now they were not able to haul it in because there were so many fish. ... When they had gone ashore, they saw a charcoal fire there, with fish on it, and bread. Jesus said to them, "Bring some of the fish that you have just caught." So Simon Peter went aboard and hauled the net ashore, full of large fish, a hundred fifty-three of them; and though there were so many, the net was not torn.
> (John 21:3-6, 9-11 NRSV)

In an aligned congregation, you should be able to trace the steps backward from each operational activity. You should be able to see how the activity connects to the action plan and how it can add to the measured accomplishment of an Objective. Objectives are designed to meet goals that flow from the purpose of a unit. The Purpose of that unit is to make a significant contribution to the accomplishment of the Strategic Direction of the congregation. When all this is working together, the Core Values are honored, there is an effective pursuit of the Mission and the Vision is alive. When implementation follows a focused plan, there is consistency, momentum for growth and judicious use of resources.

If it is true that nothing good comes from confusion, then congregational leaders must learn how to differentiate between governance and operations. Only then can they navigate freely and decisively within their given roles. The "jigsaw puzzle" comes together when a congregation has prepared itself and manages a process with the proper alignment of governance and operations.

When you spend time to plan the work, you are able to effectively work the plan.

We believe it is important to establish two different groups within a congregation: one dedicated only to governance, and the other dedicated only to operations. If a congregation chooses to have only one leadership group, it is still important to separate the governance and operations functions.

In a congregation structured with only one leadership group, meetings often take on an operational format. Except for the officers of a congregation (president, vice-president, secretary, and treasurer), virtually everyone at the table fills a staff function. We define staff as anyone who has responsibility for leading programmatic ministry. The chairpersons of all the programmatic ministries are responsible for a particular area of ministry. That means they fill staff positions albeit as volunteers. They tend to think in sixty day loops – what happened in the last thirty days and what will happen in the next thirty. The agendas are, in large part, operational in nature. For example, the Chairpersons might report on what was done in the last month and what activities will be done in the upcoming month. Chairpersons often serve because of a special fondness for the ministry they lead. Consequently, they have little time, and often little inclination, to focus on governance, which is about long range, strategic thinking and decision-making concerning the ministry of the entire congregation.

God is not a god of confusion for His people. Confusion causes problems. We must do away with structure that contributes to confusion. We should seek structures that support Spirit-led stewards living their mission as the body of Christ in the world.

Therefore, friends, select from among yourselves seven men of good standing, full of the Spirit and of wisdom, whom we may appoint to this task, while we, for our part, will devote ourselves to prayer and to serving the word.

Acts 6:3-4 (NRSV)

Chapter 5

The Church Is The People

*Faith is the first factor in a life
devoted to service. Without it,
nothing is possible. With it,
nothing is impossible.*

Mary McLeod Bethune

STEWARDS

The mission of the church is the mission of Christ. Christ told His church that it would have a missional focus (Matt 28:19-20). That mission was given to people – people who are called out by God to be His church.

We are the church, and therefore we are Spirit-led stewards living our mission as the body of Christ in the world. As stewards, our primary calling is to serve the world in the name of Christ so that an ever growing number of people are connected to Jesus. Stewards of the congregation are the body of Christ who, in faith and with conscious risk, invest themselves and their resources in order to enhance the mission of the Gospel. The focus of the stewards' missional efforts is not their wants and desires, but what Christ wants for those the church serves.

GOVERNANCE BOARD

Those who come together as Stewards are the governing body of a congregation (e.g., Congregational Assembly, General Assembly and Voters Assembly). However, it is simply not possible for all the Stewards to meet together often enough and long enough to determine how the congregation can best carry out its mission. Therefore they elect representatives who attend to this important work on their behalf. These elected leaders comprise the Governance Board. They are responsible to all of the Stewards and are tasked with setting the Strategic Direction, providing oversight and cultivating and ensuring effective stewardship. The Governance Board leads a powerful, ethical and responsible pursuit of the congregation's mission.

SENIOR PASTOR

The Senior Pastor has a unique leadership role in a congregation. The Senior Pastor is the only person who has a role in both governance and operations (we will explore this more in the next two chapters). As such, he/she must fulfill several critical functions:

- The Senior Pastor is responsible to the Governance Board and thus the congregation for leading operational staff in bringing about measurable progress with regard to the Strategic Direction set by the Board.

- The Senior Pastor is also called by God to be a prophetic voice to the congregation. This means he/she not only proclaims the good news of the Gospel but must also, when necessary, speak a word of law to individuals or the whole congregation when they have strayed from the path of God's Word. When the congregation is aligned with the Word of God, the Senior Pastor is honor bound to accept direction and oversight from the Governance Board and to be responsible for the implementation of the Strategic Direction.

- The Senior Pastor continually explores new approaches to ministry and the administration of a congregation. He/She will find it necessary from time to time to offer advice and sometimes even instruction to the Board and the Stewards regarding the effective and efficient structure of the congregation.

STAFF

The people who lead operational efforts in a congregation are staff. They may be professional, or they may be volunteers. Nevertheless, they fulfill staff obligations and responsibilities. Volunteer staff may include the Sunday school teachers, youth counselors, visitation team, ushers and all who carry out a programmatic ministry. While they are significant leaders for the congregation, they should not set policy or do any other Governance Board work. Their task is not to establish the Strategic Direction but to ensure that the resources of the congregation are utilized to bring about the envisioned future as established by the Board. They are in the trenches of mission and ministry operating the day in day out service. And staff must work to avoid the silo effect – working on their own without awareness of the other workers – while bringing about a cooperative, collaborative approach to their work.

THE SERVED

The Served are those who utilize and benefit from the ministries chosen by the congregation to fulfill its mission. These ministries may include spiritual care, visitation, worship services, education classes, food pantry, mission trips, parenting classes and a host of other ministries that benefit people. Obviously, members of the congregation are "the served," but a congregation must also serve non-members in order to be true to a missional focus.

MEMBERS

All congregations have members, and all members should be Stewards or at least Stewards in training. Unfortunately, too many see membership as being related to benefits and privileges rather than stewardship. Church membership must be aligned with stewardship.

We encountered a congregation that averaged between 900-950 people in worship on a weekend. The members of this congregation totaled 650. When asked about this unusual trend, the Senior Pastor said, "Anyone can participate in worship or other ministries without being a member. Membership is about responsibility and accountability." In this congregation, members saw themselves as stewards of the congregation's ministry to the Served.

While Stewards are also served within the congregation, that service is to enhance their stewardship, not simply to address their wants or needs. Furthermore, they must not think like the Served when making decisions about the governance and the Strategic Direction of the congregation. The Strategic Direction is about what God wants His church to be, the visible presence of Christ in the world. That is especially true for those who are not yet connected to Jesus. It is this *being* that should guide congregational decision-making. This understanding is vitally important for those elected to serve on the Governance Board.

All of the stewards are served, but not all of the served are stewards.

When a Board thinks more like "the served" rather than "stewards," it is impossible to accomplish the church's mission. Here are some actual situations where the Board behaved more like "the served" than "stewards."

- A congregation conducted a successful fund drive that raised $75,000 to repair their pipe organ and then had to close the church three years later.

- A congregation worshipping twenty people on a Sunday morning had thirty acres in a rapidly growing neighborhood, but their number one priority was to repair the steeple.

- A congregation received an estate gift of $300,000, and the only investment the Board could lead the congregation to agree upon was to give $100,000 to the cemetery fund.

It is a natural tendency for any organization to become in-
wardly focused. In many congregations the membership tends to
slide toward the side of being served rather than being stewards.
No structural change will be able to revitalize the church if the
elected leadership are not primarily stewards of God's grace for
those within and outside of church membership.

The Board and the Senior Pastor have to lead the congregation
by example. We do not believe the congregation can transform
members to be stewards by decree, coercion or cajoling. Board
members that function as Stewards are committed to spiritual
leadership. They themselves honor the values of the congregation
and personally live Christ's vision for the church. They dramatically, consistently and repeatedly align themselves with God's plan
for their church. Five things demonstrate this dramatic alignment
with God's plan:

1. The Board members come together in prayer and
   dialog with each other and with other Stewards to
   determine what God is calling the congregation to
   be in the world. They seek God's vision to revitalize
   the Vision for their congregation.

2. The Board members work toward concordance
   among themselves and do not expect consensus
   among the congregation.

3. The Board ensures that church members are served
   with love and a high quality of nurturing and that
   these members are empowered in their relationships for said mission.

4. The Board guarantees that those who are not yet
   members and may never become members are offered the same love and high quality of nurturing
   as the current members.

5. The Board expects and embraces resistance from
   current members because of number 4. The Board
   recognizes that it is natural for members to feel a
   loss by no longer being the sole focus of the mission. This resistance is healthy and may produce
   new awareness within the congregation.

Another reality which needs to be considered exists in all organizations. It is the 80/20 Principle, also known as the Paretto Principle. This familiar formula asserts that 20% of the inputs and efforts of the system account for 80% of the outputs and results, and the remaining 80% of the inputs and efforts will produce only 20% of the outputs and results.

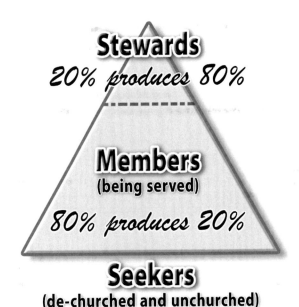

In other words, 20% of the membership of a church will produce 80% of the results for the congregation, while 80% of the members will only produce 20%. If you have ever engaged in a capital campaign, you have probably encountered this formula.

When we discuss the 80/20 Principle with congregational leaders, we often hear, "What we need to do is increase the 20% to 25% or 30%." However, this principle is not something to overcome; it is something that states the truth about your congregation. Utilizing this principle will make you more aware of your structure. In other words, if you spend time enhancing and improving the 20%, you will dramatically increase the output. However, it will take great effort, time and resources to increase the output of the 80%. Spending significant time, effort and resources improving the Stewards of the congregation will have greater results than the same effort spent on those who only desire to be served. The long term results will be improved service for "the served." More importantly, the size of the organization will grow, thus increasing the numbers within the percentages. Twenty percent of a membership of 300 is greater than twenty percent of a membership of 200. Do you want more people actively involved in your congregation? Connect more people to Jesus. Look beyond your current 80% membership to the ones who are de-churched or un-churched. This growth, while slower, is more sustainable.

The 80/20 Principle reveals a challenge concerning governance. The Stewards behave like owners of a business. They invest time and effort in the congregation in order to accomplish the purpose of the church. They want both the member and the seekers to be served.

Eighty percent of the members behave less like Stewards (owners) and more like the Served (customers). You can usually tell the difference. When the parking lot is full on a Sunday morning, the Steward says with excitement, "Look at all the cars. I had to cross the street to find a spot to park. Isn't it wonderful?" Those who think only like the Served say with disappointment, "Look at all the cars. I had to park across the street to find a place to park. Isn't it awful?"

Most congregations are structured so that all members have a vote in governance. We think it is important to remember that a member who only wants to be served will not want the stewards to spend resources on the seekers. If the congregation listens only to the Served, it will continue to shrink. It is not just an important organizational principle; it is a spiritual tenet. Jesus said, "…just as the Son of Man came not to be served but to serve, and to give his life a ransom for many" (Matthew 20:28 NRSV).

All the sons and daughters of this world – the de-churched, the un-churched, the lost, the forgotten, the elite, the powerful – are God's people. Like the lost son, the lost coin and the lost sheep, God loves them and commands His church to go and find them.

The Board, the Senior Pastor, the staff and staff volunteers, the members, and the Served, all are people of God, created, redeemed and sanctified for their role in the body of Christ. But it is the heart of those who are stewards that must guide the ministry of the congregation; it is the steward who seeks to carry out God's missional plan of reconciling the world to himself through the redemptive work of Jesus Christ.

*For as in one body we have
many members, and not all the
members have the same function,
so we, who are many, are one
body in Christ, and individually
we are members one of another.
We have gifts that differ
according to the grace given to us:
prophecy, in proportion to faith.*

Romans 12:4-6 (NRSV)

Chapter 6

Governance Options

*We must dare to think
"unthinkable" thoughts. We must
learn to explore all the options
and possibilities that confront
us in a complex and rapidly
changing world. We must learn
to welcome and not to fear the
voices of dissent.*

J. William Fulbright

THE ZORRO CLUB

Growing up, we applied organization to our playtime activities. I (Kurt) was president of the Zorro Club. It was not an official fan club of the popular 1960s television show. We just played at being organized. We even had officers. Allen was the vice president. Even though Carol couldn't write, she was the secretary. Bruce was the treasurer; however, he was forced to resign because his mom didn't want him to be responsible for the monthly five cent dues. Our organizational procedures were "made up," yet we instinctively behaved the way we imagined adults would. Our collective, albeit brief, experience formed the implicit guidelines for the club. It was great summer fun, especially when the meetings would spontaneously erupt into sword fighting. Almost 50 years have gone by and the Zorro Club lives on in church structures – structures that follow old and predictable patterns.

Congregations can also be organized with the collective understandings and assumptions of the leadership. They follow patterns of behavior established by previous generations even when it is not clear why those patterns have emerged. It is possible that Board members don't even refer to their constitution and by-laws. When asked for a copy, there is often confusion regarding location, revised copies and validity. Leaders in one congregation said, "We don't actually follow the by-laws because they don't work."

The collective understanding of the leadership also guides behaviors, regardless of the end result. Powerful group dynamics keep repeating old and inefficient patterns. We have determined a clear and explicit framework for congregational structure that will result in being the church rather than playing church.

Whether it is a Church Council, Vestry, Board of Directors or other structure, the governing group must recognize its responsibility to apply principled and focused guidance for a healthy and growing church. Sometimes governing groups have a significant role in operations, managing and implementing programmatic ministries (like a Church Council). These groups often become so focused upon the day-to-day workings of the church that they ignore or have little time for the full breadth of their fiduciary responsibility, which is to act in the capacity of a steward of another's rights, assets and well being.

A governing group exists on behalf of the Stewards of the congregation and should speak as one voice. The governing group should be planning for the future – a future which would see the expansion of the stewardship of each and every member of the congregation. This is ministry – connecting more and more people to Christ. In the very small congregation, the members (voters assembly or congregational meeting) provide governance and do not need representation such as a board. In this case, the voters meeting or congregational assembly meets monthly and provides the leadership role. This approach often deteriorates into inordinately long meetings focused not just on operational decisions but often the most trivial of operational issues like the brand of coffee pot to purchase and how many. This is an example of something that is not a leadership, steward-level decision.

GOVERNANCE OPTIONS

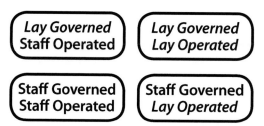

Missional congregational structure hinges on the two functions of governance and operations with a third component being people. "Who governs?" and "Who operates?" are the defining questions. With those three variables in mind, congregations may have the following structures.

Staff Governed – Staff Operated

In some cases the ministry of the congregation is driven by a Senior Pastor and his/her staff. The Senior Pastor is the visionary who may very well have given birth to the congregation and has been at the helm for a number of years. He/She has been instrumental in bringing on other paid staff who are willing to buy into his/her vision and follow it. There may be some members who serve in a Board capacity, but often, decisions about the strategic direction and the needed execution come from the staff.

Staff Governed – Lay Operated

This model comes from a by-gone era when a Pastor tended to be one of the most educated people in the congregation. The Pastor often determined what needed to be done in order for the congregation to move forward. He/she assigned responsibilities to various members of the congregation and expected them to follow through. This may still be the case in small, "family-sized" congregations or even in some larger congregations with dynamic pastoral leadership.

Lay Governed – Lay Operated

In cases where the Pastor is seen primarily as the spiritual leader of the congregation, the administration of ministries is left up to the direction of and implementation by the members of the congregation. The Pastor is engaged in preaching, teaching, visitation, chaplaincy and administration of Word and Sacraments. The members not only run the programmatic ministries, but they also set the Strategic Direction. This approach often takes the form of a Church Council. Unfortunately, because Church Councils are basically a staff gathering albeit volunteer staff, the primary focus tends to be on operational issues. Most Church Councils have a sixty-day window. They talk about what they have done in the last thirty days and what they plan to do in the next thirty days. They tend to have little time to attend to long-term strategic thinking. Consequently, their programmatic ministries are built on what they believe their individual Boards should do, with too little attention, if any, to what God is calling the congregation to be.

Lay Governed – Staff Operated

This model emphasizes the ministry as belonging to the congregation and its members. The Senior Pastor and other staff are there to serve these Spirit-led stewards as they live out their mission as the body of Christ in the world. This model provides strong ownership of the ministry by the members and dynamic utilization of the gifts of the Senior Pastor and the paid/volunteer staff. We believe this model best serves to maintain the effective alignment of governance and operations in a congregation.

Topic	LAY GOVERNED-LAY OPERATED (similar to a Church Council)	LAY GOVERNED-STAFF OPERATED (similar to a Governance Board)
Strategic Thinking	Yes, in addition to operational management when time allows.	Yes, primary responsibility.

Topic	LAY GOVERNED-LAY OPERATED (similar to a Church Council)	LAY GOVERNED-STAFF OPERATED (similar to a Governance Board)
Pastoral Accountability	Usually unclear. Often expected to be accountable for results in areas of ministry where the authority has been given to an elected/appointed group.	Accountable to the Governance Board for predetermined outcomes.
Implementation of the Plan	Council sets and implements ends and means.	Board sets ends. Staff sets means.
Staff Supervision and Oversight	Multiple lines of supervision and authority.	Single line of supervision and authority.
Financial Management	Elected treasurer and financial secretary assume responsibility for oversight of financial expenditures within budgetary limitations. Council appoints a financial reviewer or auditor.	Elected or appointed treasurer or business manager works under the direction of the Senior Pastor for oversight of financial expenditures within budgetary limitations. Board receives and scrutinizes regular financial reports through the Senior Pastor. The Board appoints a financial reviewer or auditor.
Crisis Management	Responding to and resolving crises may fall to a variety of people within the congregation.	The responsibility of the Senior Pastor is to inform the Board of all current and potential crises and work within established policies.

Topic	LAY GOVERNED-LAY OPERATED (similar to a Church Council)	LAY GOVERNED-STAFF OPERATED (similar to a Governance Board)
Leadership Development	Leaders are developed by operational groups in order to accomplish their ministries, after they are elected to an office.	Leaders are developed by the Board as potential Board members. Pastor and staff develop leaders aligned with the Strategic Direction.
Alignment of Governance and Operations	Mixing of both because responsible for both.	Clear division of responsibility: Governance to the Stewards and the Board; Operations to the Senior Pastor and the Staff.
Representation of Stewards and the Served	Because there is dual responsibility of governance and operations, there is a tendency to drift toward decisions based on the desires of the Served.	Sole responsibility of Board is to represent the desires of the steward ethos. Senior Pastor and staff are responsible for Operations.
Chairperson	President of the congregation oversees the work of the Operational Boards and represents the congregation.	Chairperson responsible for the effective work of the Board and effective communication with the Stewards.
Elections	Officers and Chairpersons of Operational Board elected by congregation.	Officers and Board members-at-large elected by the congregation.

Topic	LAY GOVERNED-LAY OPERATED (similar to a Church Council)	LAY GOVERNED-STAFF OPERATED (similar to a Governance Board)
Reporting	Individual Boards report on their activities to the Council and congregation. Senior Pastor reports information he/she deems important.	Board reports to the congregation. Pastor reports to the Board based upon predetermined requests for information from the Board.
Delegation	Council or Officers delegate authority to whomever they believe should have authority.	Board delegates to Senior Pastor. All others with authority to carry out ministry receive such authority from the Senior Pastor or someone to whom Senior Pastor has given the authority to delegate.
Budgeting	Individual ministry groups bring proposed budget to the Council/Vestry who amends and presents the budget to the congregation.	Senior Pastor and staff establish the operational plan from which a budget is developed. Board approves or rejects and finally brings to the congregation for an up or down vote.

IT REALLY NEEDS TO BE DIFFERENT

It could be argued that any of the models described above are legitimate based on certain variables, like the presence and size of professional staff and a long history of effective and efficient leadership. Certainly there are Boards functioning in a host of permutations on the above models. But while they may be functioning and giving some level of leadership to their congregations, far too many of them do not properly distinguish between governance and operations. Failing to do so, they have the tendency to spend an inordinate amount of time on operations. Even in small congregations that may indeed be Lay Governed-Lay Operated, the lay leadership needs to ask serious questions about its ability and commitment to giving adequate attention to the governance function. Otherwise, the lay leadership spends all of its time managing the ministry rather than giving leadership to the mission.

What about a growing congregation? Eventually the time required to manage the ministry of a growing congregation moves beyond the time and ability of even the most committed, skilled group of volunteer leaders.

One of the truly great benefits of Board governance in the not-for-profit world is the passion and commitment that individuals bring to the table. It is incredibly powerful. The intent is to provide the congregation with wisdom from such expertise. If not properly structured, that is if governance and operations are not properly distinguished, that passion and that wisdom can lead the Board into micro-management.

We believe that Aligned Governance and Operations is the best structure for congregations in mission. If you plan to grow as faithful stewards of the mission of Christ, if you anticipate growth and expansion and if you want to be more effective and more efficient with the resources God has given you, learn to practice Aligned Governance and Operations. Structure your congregation for mission. Structure matters!

Most new concepts are met with resistance, especially when changes alter a fundamental view of life. We are aware of the concerns and resistance regarding governance by policy. We have learned to listen carefully because there is always a kernel of truth in all resistance. Also, for every idea there is often another opposite and valid opinion. There are, however, a few myths that need to be exposed.

MYTHS REGARDING ALIGNED GOVERNANCE AND OPERATIONS

Myth 1: Authority is taken away from the congregation.
Authority is not taken away; it is amplified by policies aligned with the constitution and by-laws. The congregation only gives

the Board authority to act on its behalf and specifies actions that remain with the assembly – employment and removal of the Senior Pastor, buying or selling property or approving and funding a work plan. The Board exists only at the behest of the congregation and must, by policy, actively seek the guidance of the congregation while establishing the Strategic Direction.

Myth 2: Too much authority is given to the Senior Pastor.

The authority of the Board and the authority of the Senior Pastor are clearly differentiated. Their roles are brought into balance by policies that define office and purpose. The Board oversees the Senior Pastor by establishing the Strategic Direction and clarifying parameters. The Senior Pastor shepherds the Board to ensure compliance with God's Word and church doctrine. Congregations who move to Aligned Governace and Operations actually have more detailed, written guidelines for oversight of the pastor than they had before the move.

Myth 3: Fewer members are involved.

There is actually the potential for more members to be involved. All operational positions can be filled without the cumbersome election process. There is greater flexibility to recruit, train and involve more people without having to go back to the congregation for permission to be in mission. In addition, we suggest Pastors be asked to report to the Board the number of people who are involved in the ministries of the congregation, giving the Board the chance to track this issue.

Myth 4: After the policies are written, the Board is left with little to do.

While the list of things to do is shorter, the challenges are greater and a multitude of endeavors need the Board's leadership. The next and longest chapter will elaborate on the efforts of the Governance Board.

Myth 5: The Senior Pastor is already overworked. Governance by policy adds even more work.

Debunking this myth is simple; the pastor works differently, not harder. This is also pivotal to the success of Aligned Governance and Operations. Without a shift in the Senior Pastor's work habits, the structural changes will not achieve the hoped for results (See Chapter 7).

*Moses' father-in-law said to him,
"What you are doing is not good.
Now listen to me. I will give you
counsel, and God be with you!
...You should also look for able
men among all the people, men
who fear God, are trustworthy,
and hate dishonest gain; set such
men over them as officers over
thousands, hundreds, fifties and
tens. Let them sit as judges for the
people at all times."*

Exodus 18:17-22 (NRSV)

Chapter 7

Aligned Governance and Operations

*Change does not change
tradition, it strengthens it.
Change is a challenge and an
opportunity, not a threat.*

Prince Phillip, Duke of Edinburgh

Aligned Governance and Operations significantly increases effective steward leadership by establishing a group dedicated solely to governance. Without this exclusive focus, the congregation will continue to work on things that are urgently important and neglect the things that are important but not urgent. In this chapter we outline Board activities that keep them focused on the future, anticipating the guidance of the Holy Spirit. Remember in Chapter 3 we outlined the development stages of governance.

They are Cultural Context, Strategic Direction and Stewardship. Imagine what your congregation would become if the leadership continually engaged the Word of God, one another and their community as they looked for "a still more excellent way" (1 Corinthians 12:31).

A true Governance Board will be more proactive than most congregational leadership groups are used to. The work of setting the Strategic Direction and establishing the parameters within which ministry in the congregation may be conducted requires a great deal of study, reflection, prayer, dialog and decision-making. It is not simply a matter of deciding how to fulfill what the members of a congregation want for themselves and their families. It is about determining the right direction for a ministry that honors Christ and brings more people into a relationship with Him for their salvation.

All of this requires Governance Boards to proactively consider and intentionally engage on a regular basis in the discussion and development of issues like the following.

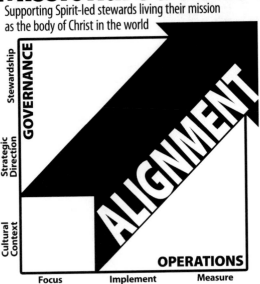

Cultural Context
- Community Relations
- Demographic Research

Strategic Direction
- Future Exploration
- Discovery Dialogs
- Future Direction

Stewardship
- Fiduciary Responsibility
- Board Education
- Norms
- Leadership Recruitment
- Management and Oversight of the Senior Pastor
- Development of Spirit-led Stewards

Cultural Context

To work on Cultural Context, a Board first needs to spend time with demographic information about its community and its own membership. It will need to hear from its membership about the cultures in which they live, work and play during the week. In addition, a Board should consider the culture of Christianity in its community and, where appropriate, its church body.

COMMUNITY RELATIONSHIPS
It is the responsibility of the Board to develop policies and procedures that ensure the nurturing of relationships with community leaders and the people who represent the neighborhood,

however your community is defined. The opportunity to meet with and discuss common concerns and shared interests is a valuable activity for the congregation. We will discuss one aspect of this later in Community Leader Dialog. The Board might decide to invite other people to come to a portion of the regular meeting to engage in dialog about the community. One meeting could involve business people, another could include social service agencies, and still others might invite the Neighborhood Watch, school officials or city/county planners.

The leadership of the congregation develops and sustains an awareness of its Cultural Context. It is the responsibility of the Governance Board to cultivate a keen awareness of the congregation's community and to assess the effectiveness and relevance of the mission. Board activity that develops cultural context includes the following:

- Dialog with key community leaders
- Assessment of future changes in the culture that may have a negative or positive effect upon the mission
- Assessment of the impact the congregation is having on the lives of individuals in the community and the community as a whole
- The research of current and future trends in the community that will provide a threat or opportunity for the congregation to accomplish its mission
- Demographic Research

Strategic Direction

Setting the Strategic Direction may be the most obvious activity that comes to mind when people think about what a Board does. The development of the Strategic Direction is an involved process. It draws information from Cultural Context. It engages a wide variety of people through surveys, focus groups, interviews, steward dialog sessions and other methodologies. It is informed by the current internal strengths and weaknesses of the congregation and the external opportunities and threats. It is shaped by Vision, which is influenced by the desire to build stewardship within the members of the congregation.

FUTURE EXPLORATION

It is essential that the Board has sufficient time to have a dialog about the future. The Board's responsibility is to ensure a relevant and sustainable future for the congregation; therefore, it must continually seek to understand the future and be proactive into the future. This process is not reactive to external trends and developments. It is proactive awareness and a readiness to implement God's vision into a transient society. The Board should determine how the Word of God will have a decisive impact on the congregation and community. If the church of Christ is to create new community aligned with the Kingdom of God, it needs to initiate proactive leadership instead of reactive adaptation.

The Board can ask the Senior Pastor to share research and personal observations about the future of congregational life in the next generations. The Board can initiate its own study by reading about the future or external expert predictions. The Board can simply draw on the insights and intuitions of its members and talk about the future. Healthy Board dialog is not looking for answers; it is reflecting on observations and giving prayerful attention to what is happening. Having a better description of the culture prepares the Board to establish a clear, proactive policy that will guide the organization in the way the Holy Spirit is leading. Don't be surprised to find God already preparing a need specifically suited for your congregation.

DISCOVERY DIALOGS

Discovery dialogs are geared to help the Board learn from the wisdom of other people as it works to set the Strategic Direction. These people may be of different theological persuasions. Nevertheless, important things can be learned by being in conversation with others. The following are five such types of conversation in which the Board can engage.

Stewards Dialog

A couple of times a year, the Board should invite four or five representatives from steward segments (by age groups, years of membership, giving levels, roles such as parents of young children or teens or former presidents of the congregation) to join them for a conversation. These steward dialogs should be 45 minutes in length and consist of two or three questions. These questions should be based on the steward ethos— "How can the congregation best serve the ministry of Jesus Christ in the world?" It will often be necessary to help the guests stay focused in this direction because the tendency will be to slide to what they want in their role as "the served." Listen. Do not argue or debate. Keep them focused on the stewardship issue. When the 45 minutes are up, thank them for their time and have someone offer a prayer for them and their commitment to the ministry of the congregation. When they have left, the Board should have a discussion guided by this question: "What are the implications of what we have just heard for the ministry of our congregation?"

Denominational Dialog

Seeking information from other Christians can be a wonderful addition to the Board's attempts to explore possibilities. If there is a clear connection to a denomination, the Board can invite the Senior Pastor and the primary lay leader from three congregations of your denomination to join you for a 45 minute conversation. This conversation should revolve around three questions:

- What do you see as the mission of a (your denomination) congregation in this community?
- How did you come to that understanding?
- How do you best exemplify that?

Do not argue or debate. Listen. Ask questions for clarity. When finished, thank them and have someone offer a word of prayer for their ministries. When your guests leave, hold a discussion about what you heard and what the implications are for the ministry of your congregation.

Other Christian Dialog

The Board can invite the Senior Pastor and primary lay leaders of the closest Christian congregations of other denominations to meet with the Board. Use the same time frame and basically the same process.

- What do you see as the mission of a Christian congregation in this community?
- How did you come to that understanding?
- How do you best exemplify that?

Do not argue or debate. Listen. Probe for clarity. Thank them and have a word of prayer for their ministries. When your guests leave, hold a discussion about what you heard and what the implications are for the ministry of your congregation.

Community Leadership Dialog

Considering the importance of cultural context in the governance process, it would be wise to hear from the community. There are a number of ways to do this, but one in particular is to invite the Mayor or a City Council person from your area to attend the Board meeting once a year. Again, this is not a long session—45 minutes should be enough. Ask these questions:

- What is your vision for our community?
- How should a Christian congregation like ours best support your vision?

Listen! Do not argue. Allow them to ask questions of your Board. Close the meeting with a prayer for the community. When he/she is gone, hold a discussion about the implications of what you heard for the ministry of your congregation.

Judicatory Dialog

If your congregation is a part of a denomination, there is a good chance that you have an elected or appointed leader of your local judicatory (presbytery, district, diocese or synod). Invite that person to join you for a 45-minute session. Ask questions like:

- What is your vision for our judicatory?
- What do you believe a congregation like ours can do to help bring about that vision?

Once again, the idea is to listen, not debate. Ask for clarity. When the time is up, express your gratitude. Have someone say a word of prayer for the judicatory and your guest's leadership. When he/she has departed, talk about the implications. Gathering insight by allowing itself to be informed and influenced by others is one way a board can keep from becoming myopic and insular in its thinking and thus limited in clarifying its vision. These dialog sessions will greatly assist the Governance Board in expanding its ability to consider new options.

ESTABLISHING FUTURE DIRECTION

Every time the board engages in a high-level dialog regarding its cultural context or strategic direction it increases its shared awareness. This awareness and insight optimizes the board's ability to establish and refine the Strategic Direction Policies. The Bible studies, demographic studies, community and church dialogs will guide the board's thinking when they establish Core Values, Mission, Vision, Critical Targets and Corporate Goals. These policies will be fully discussed in chapter ten.

Stewardship

Stewardship is a willingness to accept responsibility for the enhancement and expansion of the mission. It is about recognizing who the "owner" of the ministry is and what it means to be a steward on behalf of the owner. Stewardship within the governance function also has a teaching component. As mentioned in a previous chapter, members of a congregation are both "stewards" and "the served." Part of the responsibility of a Governance Board is to consistently help members recognize their call to stewardship and to grow in their abilities to serve the mission in this way. They need to realize that when they are served by the ministry of the congregation, it is not simply to meet their needs but to encourage and equip them as Stewards.

Ultimately, the Governance Board's responsibility to the

Stewards is to bring about a strong, powerful, ethical pursuit of the congregation's mission. There is nothing simple about doing this and especially about doing it well. It takes time and effort. Perhaps you do not really have the time but you can "make some of the meetings," or you think it is just a small not-for-profit and "How hard can it be?" If you are doing it because "no one else will," then serving on the Board is probably not for you. The missional congregation requires Board members who are passionate, dedicated and self-sacrificing because the mission has eternal consequences.

FIDUCIARY RESPONSIBILITY

When you serve as a member of the Governance Board, there is a fiduciary responsibility to the congregation. It is a relationship imposed by law where someone has voluntarily agreed to act in the capacity of a trustee of another's rights, assets and well being. This role requires that the Board member follow the governing principles of good faith, loyalty, utmost care, integrity, full disclosure and avoidance of a conflict of interest.

Good Faith

The Board member is obligated to carry out the responsibilities with the utmost degree of good faith. The member gives undivided service to the interest of the congregation and its mission. The term "good faith" has been interpreted as the imposition of an obligation to act reasonably so as to avoid negligence while handling the congregation's interests.

Utmost Care

The Board member has a duty to investigate all information and assumptions upon which decisions and policy are made. You must ensure that the best information is provided to the congregation.

Integrity

The Board member is acting with the highest Christian standards of soundness and character. It means the agent must act with openness and honesty.

Full Disclosure

The Board member must give full disclosure of all material facts, either known or reasonably discoverable, which could in any way influence the congregation's decisions and actions.

Conflict of Interest

If the Board member should find himself/herself in a position of conflicting interests (acting for two parties at the same time), he/she must disclose the dual agency.

BOARD EDUCATION

Not every Board meeting will necessarily have an education session. Board education is about helping individual members of the Board, as well as the Board as a group, to become better at the job of leading a strong, powerful, ethical pursuit of the congregation's mission. Here are important educational topics for the Board:

Finance

Virtually every not-for-profit Board could benefit from a yearly tutorial on how to read and understand financial statements.

Reaching a Decision

Boards should learn various methods for making decisions. They may agree upon a preferred process, or they may determine a different process depending on the decision to be made.

Board Dialog

The Board should know the difference between debate, discussion and dialog. They could even practice using these different approaches for appropriate topics.

Managing Conflict

Successful Boards learn to manage conflict and predetermine the approach they would like to use. This is an important step because virtually every productive group has conflict at some level. Whether you call it a disagreement or an argument, all groups need to be able to go "toe-to-toe" to discover how they can be most effective. Being able to manage conflict as it arises, rather than waiting until it has gotten so advanced it needs "resolution" is the preferred proactive approach.

Governance

A yearly booster shot of Aligned Governance and Operations has proven helpful to many of our clients. It is not unusual for the members of the Governance Board to decide that once they have their governance manual in place and have done one Board orientation, they need no further development in their skills. We have observed that two things happen with those Boards. Either they call someone to come in and help them get back on track or they drift away from aligned governance and begin to return to being a management Board.

Oversight

Boards sharpen their skills for oversight by learning what to look for in the organization. They can determine what to listen for in an operational report. They can rehearse the questions they should be asking. Assessment for the success of the mission is also a helpful education topic.

NORMS

Boards naturally develop normative behaviors. There are many unspoken rules of how things get done, when to arrive at meetings, how to dress for meetings, how much humor is acceptable or how much incompetence will be tolerated. Some rules are helpful, but some are not. These silent rules may determine what topics are never discussed. Group pressure may keep new members "in line" without a word spoken. These powerful group dynamics will continue until they are openly and directly discussed.

Productive Boards identify positive, implicit norms and write explicit policy for Board guidelines. By articulating norms, Board members are basically saying to each other, "This is how we will be together as we work for the sake of the kingdom." Through this process, Board members come to know what is expected of them and what they can expect of each other. Common expectations diminish the number and intensity of incidents of conflict. Norms also hold up appropriate expectations of those who are giving leadership to the congregation. Things like attendance at worship and Bible study are important, yet we know many who serve on Boards are less than consistent in these practices, especially their attendance at Bible study. Do you expect the Board to speak with one voice once there has been adequate dialog and a decision has been made? Unless there is an articulated norm about

> ### *Conflict is inevitable, enemies are an option.*
> *"Timeless Truths" by Les Stroh*

"one voice," it is hard to hold all members accountable for that behavior. Building a set of norms is one way to be proactive in strengthening community. A strong community always works better together than one that "just gets along."

The following are ten norms that we recommend for effective Board process:

1. Be Here.

If Jesus could have birthdays and leave footprints, His followers could learn to be in the moment, fully available for each other.

2. Say it here.

This is the time and place to get it all out in the open.

3. Keep it here.

Confidentiality fosters an environment of security and openness.

4. Speak for self about self.

Although others may feel as you do, they are not in the room and are therefore unable to speak. Your message is important, even if you are alone in your opinion.

5. Disagree openly and support those who disagree.

The best ideas come from the selection of two or more alternatives. If someone is willing to risk being different, the group needs to respond with support. This will ensure future disagreement. (Conflict does not come from voicing disagreement. It is more

likely to come from people who have not been heard
or respected for their opinions. When dialog is cut
off, passive aggressive behavior builds into eventual
conflict.)

6. Get your needs met.

Don't be uncomfortable in a meeting. Ask for what you
need in order to be productive. People have different
work styles. The meeting can be productive even if
some people are standing or pacing. Speak up if the
room is too cold/hot or too bright/dark.

7. Don't ask a question when making a statement.

This is an effective way to reduce the length of
meetings. Many questions are merely discussion
starters. Cut to the chase. Express your thoughts first.

8. Connect every agenda item to the Strategic Direction.

If the agenda item does not improve the church's ability
to accomplish the mission, don't address it.

9. Speak with one voice.

When a decision has been made, even if there was
considerable disagreement in reaching the agreement,
speak as one voice.

10. Pray throughout the meeting.

Pray at the beginning and at the end. Pray when there
is something to be thankful for. Pray when you are
confused. Stop and pray. Break into spontaneous prayer
with the sword of the Spirit, which is the Word of God.

LEADERSHIP RECRUITMENT

The Governance Board has a responsibility to develop the
servant Stewards of the congregation in order to ensure successful and sustained leadership in the years to come. The Board, not
just the nominating committee, should invest significant energy
in leadership development so that the people who replace current
members are bringing greater capacity and competency to the

Board. Here are a few suggestions on how to maintain a high level of leadership on the Board.

Establish a long list of potential candidates. Use the established policy on Governance Board criteria for membership to guarantee a qualified list. Once you have established the list, develop a strategy for how the Board will become better acquainted with these candidates and how the candidates will come to recognize service on the Board as a worthy investment of their time. Here are some possible strategies:

1. Develop a list of men and women who have potential to become governing leaders and pray for them regularly.

2. Invite one or two people from the candidate list to a couple of Board meetings. Provide introductions and a time of fellowship.

3. Meet with a potential member for lunch or coffee to talk about the work of the Board and to explore his/her interest in serving.

4. Spend time talking about potential Board members and pray that they might be led to serve.

5. Think in terms of identifying potential Board members two to four years before they might serve. Talented people are often committed to other groups and projects "right now." They may be willing to serve in two or three years when current commitments have been fulfilled, especially when given advance notice of your interest in them.

6. Inform people who are being nominated for a leadership role as far in advance as possible and ask them to prayerfully consider the opportunity. Give them a specific time frame for their decision.

7. Invite candidates to an annual Board dinner which would present an informal Board evaluation and would generate discussion about the future of the congregation.

8. Invite potential steward leaders into conversations about the purpose of the church and the governing

process of the church.

9. Include a social hour before governance meetings
   and encourage interaction with potential members
   who stay as guests of the meeting.

Board leadership is developed by intentional recruitment. It is
an ongoing process and should not be postponed until the annual
election process to see who might be interested and available.

MANAGEMENT AND OVERSIGHT
OF THE SENIOR PASTOR

We have consistently indicated that the primary responsibility
of the Board is governance, not operations. And we have indicated
that governance is more about leadership than management. There
are, however, two management responsibilities of the Board. First,
the Board needs to manage its own processes as it goes about its
own work. These processes might include nominations, Board education and dialogs as mentioned earlier. The second responsibility
is the management and oversight of the Senior Pastor.

We believe the oversight of the Senior Pastor belongs to the
Governance Board, not the deacons, elders or some other group
within the congregation. This oversight has to do with three key
areas.

- Progress in the Strategic Direction established
  by the Board
- Compliance with the policies established by the Board
- Oversight of the pastoral ministry

In a dance each partner has a responsibility to fulfill his/her
own separate, unique role; in so doing, he/she makes the other
partner look good. The congregation members, as the body of
Christ in a location, are responsible to their God for being stewards
of the ministry. The Senior Pastor, as a person responding to a call
from God to serve in this capacity, also has the responsibility to
make certain that the people he/she serves are true to the will of
God. At the same time, the Senior Pastor has a duty to the people
he/she is serving.

The Senior Pastor must see himself/herself as a servant to

the people of God in this time and this place. Consequently, it is legitimate for the congregation to hold the Senior Pastor accountable for those things mentioned above: progress with regard to the Strategic Direction, compliance with the governing policies and preaching and teaching in accordance with the Word of God.

Performance Appraisals

The Senior Pastor receives a performance appraisal from the Governance Board. It is amazing how many different stories we hear about performance appraisal processes, but most often we hear that it is not done. At times, we hear that it is done without any preparation and in a purely subjective way, either being so soft it gives the pastor no significant feedback about performance, or so harsh it blindsides the pastor with criticism that he/she has never heard before. There are ways to do performance appraisal properly, and we have some recommendations.

> *There is not a better way to convey a lack of appreciation for someone's efforts than to ignore them.*

The performance appraisal process should actually start twelve months before the formal appraisal takes place. The Senior Pastor and two or three Board members who have been charged with the task of conducting the appraisal should agree upon what the Pastor will attempt to accomplish in the upcoming year. That plan has three components.

First of all, the Senior Pastor's set of goals should flow from the Operational Path which the Pastor and staff have developed for the coming year. The Operational Path is created when the staff comes together and says, "This is what we intend to achieve in the next year that will move us forward with regard to the congregational Strategic Direction. We will be focused on these things." From that, the Senior Pastor can then say to the appraisal team, "Here is what I believe we can accomplish this year." Secondly, "I intend to pursue this sort of personal and/or professional growth this year." Finally, the Senior Pastor should share his/her intended approach to managing/overseeing the staff for the coming year. This plan forms the basis for the Senior Pastor's performance appraisal.

LEADERSHIP AND MANAGEMENT

Some of the above activities are more in the realm of management than leadership. The reality is that no position in an organization is 100% leadership or 100% management. Every position along the organizational structure has need of being able to determine "right things" and knowing how to do "things right." The diagram below displays that idea. The Governance Board at the far left is practically consumed with governance (leadership) but still has some operational (management) issues of its own to address. At the other end is the position which is actively engaged in action in the community and congregation. This position is primarily focused on doing things the right way. And yet, when no one else is around, the person in this position has to be able to determine what the "right things" are in order to be able to do "things right."

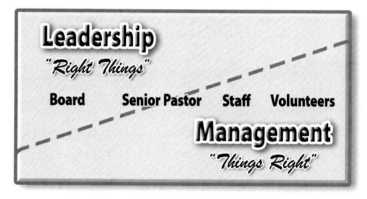

The Governance Board's primary task is governance. There are indeed some operational (management) issues it must also address. Previously, we discussed some of these (for example, Board Education, Management and Oversight of the Senior Pastor and Leadership Recruitment). Boards often become consumed with their own management details and develop an unhealthy interest in tasks. They become enthralled by operational details of the day-to-day life of the congregation; this is known as micro-management. They become distracted by the urgent, yet not always important, operational issues while neglecting the truly important, but seldom urgent, governance concerns. The short-term benefits of Board efforts in operations will not sustain the congregation. However, long-term benefits of leadership through aligned governance will be realized for decades to come.

THE ROLE OF THE SENIOR PASTOR WITHIN GOVERNANCE

The challenges a congregation faces are significantly embedded in both the church and the community. Successful planning requires more than a few adjustments of attitude and program. The current mission culture requires substantial change and Spirit-led transformation within the leadership

The need for leadership is voiced repeatedly in church journals, on websites and in books. A survey of our libraries includes the following titles (see appendix for authors and publishers):

- *An Emergent Theology for Emerging Churches*
- *The Externally Focused Church*
- *Hit the Bullseye, How Denominations Can Aim Congregations at the Mission Field*
- *Being Leaders, The Nature of Authentic Christian Leadership*
- *Power Surge, Six Marks of Discipleship for a Changing Church,*
- *The Present Future, Six Tough Questions for the Church*
- *Pastor, The Theology and Practice of Ordained Ministry*
- *Simple Church, Returning to God's Process for Making Disciples*
- *The Unnecessary Pastor*
- *Deep Change*

Three thoughts are found in all these books.

1. The fundamental thinking of congregations must change from ministry to mission.
2. The structure of a congregation must be renewed for mission.

3. Pastors must provide strong leadership in the transformation process.

The specific role of a Senior Pastor may vary depending on the rubrics of the congregation and denomination. Our thoughts are based on these beliefs:

- The ministry of the congregation belongs to the congregation. Senior Pastors and other staff people come and go, but the congregation remains. The Stewards have the responsibility of making sure the mission and ministry of the congregation are God-pleasing and contributing to God's will that "all people would be saved."

- The Senior Pastor may indeed be seen as the "shepherd of the flock who tends the sheep," but that is certainly not his/her only role; just as important is the reality that he/she is a model steward of the congregation.

- As a model steward, the Senior Pastor is largely one who equips people for the ministry of being "Spirit-led stewards living out their mission as the body of Christ in the world today."

- All aspects of the congregation's ministry have a spiritual dimension. Therefore, the Senior Pastor, as the primary staff person in the congregation, should work to ensure that all aspects of the ministry are aligned with the will of God. At some point, should the congregation ever stray from the Word of God in its direction and decision-making, the Senior Pastor needs to provide a prophetic voice.

- As human beings, Senior Pastors sometimes err and deviate from the path God has set before them. They must be accountable to the congregation based on established guidelines.

We have now explored the many strategic advantages of Aligned Governance. This structure creates a new and sustainable emphasis on governance as leadership and prepares the congregation to be dramatically effective in operations. Operations are important and, to be effective in the long run, operations must be handled by the right people in the right way. The next chapter will explore those issues.

I told them that the hand of my God had been gracious upon me, and also the words that the king had spoken to me. Then they said, "Let us start building!" So they committed themselves to the common good.

Nehemiah 2:18 (NRSV)

Chapter 8
Operations

*Men often oppose a thing merely
because they have had no agency
in planning it, or because it
may have been planned by those
whom they dislike.*

Alexander Hamilton

An effective operational structure must not only allow for, but also contribute to, the implementation of an effective Operational Path. Without a clear mission, congregations focus on activity and eventually become enslaved by it. Without clear Action Plans, congregations get poor results and wonder what went wrong with their mission. The greatest challenge of the church, comprised of mostly volunteer workers, is to maintain a consistent Operational Path aligned with the Strategic Direction. Too often we see churches go back to their Mission Statements, reworking them instead of looking honestly at their operational efforts. These problems are often literally embedded in the structure of the congregation and are repeated year in and year out regardless of their effectiveness in pursuing the stated mission. Congregations fail to bring about envisioned futures when leadership is unwilling or incapable of aligning their behaviors (operations) with their Strategic Direction, resulting in the failure of the congregation to do the same.

We will explore the developmental stages of Operations: Focus, Implement and Measure. Before we do that, we need to take a look at two significant components within Operations. The first is the role and function of the Senior Pastor and staff, and the second is the way operations are actually organized or structured.

We have an online survey at www.cornerstonefactor.com that asks our clients to give us information concerning their "Capacity for Vision" and their "Competency for Action." What we discovered from the first 100 organizations is that they have high scores for Strategic Direction and low scores for Operational Path. The following chart shows samples of their responses:

Strategic Direction	Disagree Strongly	Disagree	Disagree Somewhat	Agree Somewhat	Agree	Agree Strongly
This organization includes people who can assimilate complex information into one dynamic vision.	4%	23%	18%	19%	20%	11%
This organization places value on its history and past experiences.	2%	14%	5%	22%	36%	21%
The vision of this organization is insightful.	7%	15%	21%	19%	28%	10%

Operational Path	Disagree Strongly	Disagree	Disagree Somewhat	Agree Somewhat	Agree	Agree Strongly
The people of this organization are able to organize and accomplish their work sequentially without interruption or delay.	6%	36%	17%	23%	13%	4%
This organization is able to implement its plans with coordination and cooperation.	7%	20%	28%	18%	16%	8%

Operational Path	Disagree Strongly	Disagree	Disagree Somewhat	Agree Somewhat	Agree	Agree Strongly
This organization implements project evaluation throughout the project in order to make the necessary adaptations and corrections.	15%	33%	16%	25%	8%	3%

	Strategic Direction	Operational Path
Overall Percentage of Agreement	**61%**	**39%**

(Some percentages do not add up to 100% due to rounding)

The above information indicates a lack of alignment. No matter how dynamic and God-pleasing the Strategic Direction is, it cannot be achieved without an equally dynamic and God-pleasing approach to operations. A well-structured congregation has both visionary, dedicated leadership and skilled, focused management.

OPERATIONAL PATH

We find it helpful to think of operations as a path which includes Focus, Implement and Measure.

Les's mom attended a family reunion in Manhattan, Montana each summer. The family members lived in Oregon, Missouri, Montana and Washington. Les lived in Missouri. In order to get to the reunion, his parents chose a path for the trip. Sitting around the kitchen table looking at a road map, they considered the trip. They planned the path that included sightseeing, visits to relatives and other stops along the way.

Yet even after all the planning, nothing happened until they packed the car, left the driveway and headed for Montana. They knew how far they needed to go each day, and they knew whom and what they wanted to see as the journey progressed. As you might imagine, the trip never went precisely as planned. At times the auto needed repair and the schedule had to be recalculated-

stops omitted and visits canceled. Nevertheless, the Stroh family made it to the reunion every time. Determining the path to the reunion included focus, implementation and measurements.

Focus

As Alice realized while standing at the crossroads in Wonderland, if it does not matter where you are headed, then it does not matter which road you take. The Operational Path must align with the Strategic Direction established by the Governance Board. In other words, it does matter which road you take, or at least it should matter. Many congregations fail to accomplish their mission because they attempt to do too much. Effective decision-making by the Board will help establish only a few outcomes. In today's emerging culture, specialists are often valued over generalists. Even complex organizations find greater success in maintaining a narrow emphasis. By keeping all operations aligned with a few outcomes (established by the Governance Board), the congregation will gain momentum, efficiency and effectiveness. Concentrate on a few targets chosen carefully by the Board and apply virtually all resources of time, equipment, staff and prayers. Then you will begin to see results.

Just as the Board has to determine what is critical for the strategic direction, the Pastor and staff must also ensure a focused operational effort. They must be willing to let go and say no to things that may be helpful, important and even God-pleasing in favor of efforts that are God-pleasing and determined to be essential.

An example from the ministry of Jesus that illustrates this point is found in Luke 4. It is the story of Jesus going to Capernaum. He teaches the people, and "they were amazed at His teaching." He casts out demons and cures the fever of Peter's mother-in-law. As these stories are told and retold, the people bring others with all kinds of sicknesses, and Jesus lays his hands on them and heals them. One morning, Jesus goes out to find a little peace and quiet, but the people come looking for Him. "And when they came to where He was, they tried to keep Him from leaving." After all, there is more to learn, there are more people to be healed and more demons to be cast out. There is still much good ministry to be done here – much that will glorify God and honor the kingdom. But Jesus has a different focus for His ministry. "I must preach the good news of the kingdom of God to the other towns also, because that is why I was sent." Jesus said, "No" to perfectly legitimate ministry opportunities in order to focus on his primary mission – to save all the people of the world. If a congregation expects to build any momentum toward its desired future, it may have to say "No" to many ministries that have become traditional. Remember, there will always be numerous activities that seem helpful, even important; however, successful operations focus on the Board's mandate. Keep asking yourself, "Of all the things we could do in ministry, what must we do in order to most effectively focus on the targets, pursue the mission and honor the core values?"

Implement

When operational church structure succeeds, it is because people know they are in it for the long haul. Improving performance requires long-term commitment and long-term focus. The Senior Pastor must help staff members gain a clear, focused understanding of the mission. As they go about their day-to-day ministry, they need to act consistently and repeatedly in alignment with the mission. The Senior Pastor and his/her management team must ask staff members one by one to articulate the contribution they will make in moving the congregation forward along the Strategic Direction. This requires intentional time spent in supervising, giving significant attention to orientation, coaching, supporting, evaluating and empowering others.

No operational unit (staff member, staff volunteer or team) should begin the operational year without a written Operational Path for achieving its purpose that is aligned with the Strategic Direction. Management of the unit requires supervision, particularly of the staff leading the units. There should be consistent and timely reviews of the progress being made toward established goals. There should be mid-year and annual performance appraisals.

Measure

Measurable growth is the result of immeasurable grace. The value of the church is beyond measurement. Try to fathom amazing grace. You can't count the children of Abraham or measure the depth of Christ's sacrifice. The *being* of the church and its governance has limitless potential. The steward leaders are nurtured and sustained by this endless supply of hope. God's success is often fulfilled in total failure and realized among the poor and humble. Perhaps that is why some church leaders feel measurement in earthly terms is inappropriate. This is when we hear the phrase, "The church is not a business."

We believe that you cannot advance the mission without measurement. Assessment is essential for improvement. Unless you are talking about attendance, measurement is mostly neglected in the church. While attendance is the easiest to measure, it is not strategic. Effective operations measure results. People will do the things for which they are being measured. Too often we do not want to be held accountable by being measured. God is counting on us, not because He needs to, but because, as incredible as it sounds, God chooses people to carry on the mission.

Consider these five "don'ts" when it comes to measurement.

1. Don't fail to measure ministry effectiveness.
2. Don't ask how it is going if you haven't first indicated that it is important.

3. Don't ask someone to measure a result if you have not connected it specifically to the mission.

4. Don't fail to help someone understand how their efforts have impacted or failed to impact the mission.

5. Don't try to convince someone something is important if you don't plan to measure it.

Measurement and evaluation are initially difficult for a congregation. However, after establishing a few critical benchmarks, the progress or lack of it should be easy to detect. Managers initiate measurements with a small number of operational staff. In order to have an evaluation process, there needs to be an establishment of goals, objectives and action plans as mentioned in Chapter 3.

In order to help staff fully believe they are indeed making a contribution, you must be able to show them the numbers. Complimenting people on the job they did accomplishes nothing if you cannot be specific about the impact of their work. In congregational ministry there are powerful ways to measure accomplishment. A manager could say, "Because of your specific action, this person was changed in this way and to this degree." While some action plans tend to measure activity, it is best to measure results.

> *It is not possible for congregations to raise the level of excellence without cutting some ministry. This will produce focused excellence rather than a broad array of mediocrity.*

Successful missional structure includes an operational system that has skilled and focused management with specific roles. It has the ability to develop and implement a plan focused on a few essential areas of effort. Successful operations also provide evaluation and performance reviews for all staff. Without mission-aligned measurements, a congregation will not be able to determine the effectiveness of its efforts. If the measurement criteria are not focused on results, a congregation will only be able to measure busyness. Busyness is not an effective measure of true progress toward your

Strategic Direction. Busyness is too often justified with activities that we like or those at which we tend to be successful. Anyone can stay busy doing the same things over and over. However, that does not equal productivity. "Puttin' your boots in the oven, don't make 'em biscuits." Just *being* busy does not make you productive.

Evaluation that analyzes activity fails to provide the information necessary to make corrections or adaptations to your ministry. You will better know how to improve when you are measuring outcomes, the results of the activity. For instance, a measurement of busyness would ask, "How many adults have been trained as youth counselors?" The answer may be, "We have trained four. That's two more than last year." Helpful! Important! Yet to know if you have made an impact on the mission, you must ask a different question: "Are young people more connected to Jesus because of the work of our youth counselors?"

When you do what you've always done, you'll get what you always got.

Following the suggestion in Chapter 3 for establishing Strategic Direction, the Governance Board establishes Indicators of Success which tell the Board, the Senior Pastor and the staff what it would look like if these goals were being met. Indicators are not hard line goals in and of themselves. They are the talking points. Let's say Christian living is one of the Critical Targets of your congregation.

In the case of Effective Christian Living, the indicators (outcome criteria) will be different for every congregation, but some might look like the following:

- More members participating in servant events
- Increased volunteer service to the ongoing ministries of the congregation
- Increased numbers of individuals deciding to go into full time service to the church
- More young adult activity in a congregation/ campus ministry when away at college
- Higher self-reporting on inviting others to attend congregational events

After these Indicators are identified, they must then be bench-marked. Ask yourself, "What is the current level of outcome?" Once you know where you are beginning, you can measure your progress through data collections, surveys and observations. This sort of measurement tells a congregation what level of progress is being made and helps the Senior Pastor and staff know where further effort is needed.

Measurement helps determine the level of effectiveness of past efforts and also indicates what steps must be taken next. If you don't change your behaviors, you cannot expect different results.

OPERATIONAL ROLES

No congregation functions without staff, paid or volunteer. The trap is that once a position is established, it remains the same year after year, even when the Strategic Direction changes. Staff, like the budget, must always be aligned with and in support of the Strategic Direction. The following section explores the roles of Senior Pastor and Staff within Aligned Operations.

Senior Pastor

The day when the Senior Pastor served primarily as a shep-herd is over. The emerging needs of today's congregations in a post-modern culture necessitates a greater emphasis on the role of the pastor as an effective administrator. He/She should be able to focus, implement and measure the operational ministries of the congregation. Whether you are in a large congregation with professional staff or a small congregation dependent on volunteer staff, the role of the pastor remains the same. Senior Pastors are shepherds of the flock. They must be skilled and focused when it comes to managing day-to-day operational efforts, or they must find a teammate who can fulfill this role.

The Senior Pastor is an ex-officio (without vote) member of the Governance Board who provides spiritual guidance and vision for Board governance. He/she also lives in the world of operations. The Senior Pastor is the primary staff person for the congregation. He/She is accountable to the Board for ensuring that resources are being used to move the congregation forward in the Strategic Direction the Board has established. All other staff, professional or volunteer, receive authority and responsibility from the office of the Senior Pastor or another senior staff member who is directly accountable to the Senior Pastor.

The Senior Pastor as management leader is best positioned to oversee the design and implementation of the operational structure of the congregation, and to ensure it is God-pleasing. This process of establishing a clear management leader gives clarity to the entire operational effort. It keeps all operational staff, committees, task forces and volunteers clearly informed about the lines and functions of their positions. Clear lines of authority enable clear accountability. Clear accountability leads to clear and effective action. The ability to accomplish the mission is significantly reduced when there is ambiguity regarding lines of function and authority.

The Board is ultimately responsible to the congregation for governance, and as long as the Board keeps the congregation aligned with God's Word, the Senior Pastor's ministry is honor-bound to accept direction and oversight from the Board. It is only when the Board or congregation is at odds with God's Word that the Senior Pastor must step in and exercise "authority" over the congregation. Once the congregation is again aligned with God's Word, the Senior Pastor once again accepts direction and oversight from the Board.

The Senior Pastor should have the authority to establish operational plans that are effective. For example, he/she could turn everything over to a handful of leaders and empower them to accomplish the mission within the governing policies of the congregation, or he/she could assemble various task forces or standing committees who could organize themselves into action. The Senior Pastor could possibly establish a Council of Ministries that would, under his/her leadership, implement the actions necessary to support an effective pursuit of the congregation's mission. While this may seem like additional work for the Senior Pastor, the ability to maintain flexibility and agility would foster less work in the long run. Someone has to give attention to the structure and administration of a coordinated operational effort. If not the Senior Pastor, then who? To suggest that the Senior Pastor is responsible for the spiritual life of the congregation but not programmatic ministries, finances, administration and the like is to imply that certain aspects of congregational life are not spiritual. Pastors should be providing spiritual counsel and guidance to all aspects of congregational life.

Historical wisdom suggests that no one can effectively manage more than six direct reports. Consequently, an operational structure needs to multiply leadership. The Senior Pastor must judiciously select the staff (professional and volunteer) whom he/she will manage to produce the best impact on the Strategic Direction. In this way, the Senior Pastor would cultivate another level of oversight. He/she must inspire the staff to not only carry out their ministry but to also empower and manage other people in order to accomplish the vision established by the Board of Directors.

A Senior Pastor needs to set aside at least 20 hours a year for one-to-one supervision of each of the people who report directly to him/her. This is approximately two-and-one-half work days a year per person. This does not include staff meetings. These are one-to-one, scheduled, supervision sessions. If the Senior Pastor has six direct reports, it will average out to a minimum of fifteen days a year. It is imperative that a supervisor have no more than a half dozen direct reports. When the work load exceeds this, one of two things happens. Either the supervisor does indeed supervise all direct reports and gets at none of the other things he/she is supposed to accomplish, or, and this is the most likely, no real supervision takes place.

Staff

In the past church structure has relied upon elected Boards and Committees to carry out congregational operations. This process, as directed in the by-laws, requires annual elections, terms of service and a specified number of members. For many congregations this has become cumbersome and unproductive. While some Boards flourish, others flounder. The annual elections could have a dramatic impact on the operations. In smaller congregations everyone knows the people whom they elect to the Council. In larger congregations members end up voting for people they do not know. Consequently, many congregations have wisely modified their constitutions to eliminate elections for operational servants. This builds greater flexibility in the operational structure. When this reorganizing of operational structure is developed and managed by the Senior Pastor or his/her appointed representative, the process and progress can move quickly and efficiently. The Senior

Pastor can spend less time managing the structure and more time adapting and improving its productivity.

All people who carry out operational duties are operational staff. Some congregations have professional staff in addition to their Pastor, but all congregations operate with volunteer staff. Sunday school teachers, altar guild members, ushers and choir members all provide programmatic ministry services; therefore, they are operational staff.

In principle, there is no difference between a professional staff and a volunteer staff. Both the professional and volunteer staff are expected to "focus, implement and measure" their own performance. Both paid and volunteer staff are more effective when they know and understand their level of authority, the limit of their responsibility and, finally, to whom they report. Both should be accountable to the Senior Pastor (or someone to whom he/she has delegated management responsibility) and ultimately to the Board and the Congregation.

The Senior Pastor must choose a manageable, effective number of professional staff or lay leaders (volunteer staff) whom he/she will empower for mission. In a multi-staff situation, it is important that the pastor validate the ministry of the volunteer staff in the same way he/she validates the professional staff.

OPERATIONAL STRUCTURE

To make effective use of staff, there must be a determination about how the congregation will go about its work. That means the Senior Pastor must establish an Operational Structure with the intent of bringing life to the Strategic Direction of the congregation. This structure establishes Units for each programmatic ministry area (Outreach, Education, Worship, Discipleship, etc.). An Operational Unit is responsible for its assigned programmatic ministry. Units are led by professional staff members or by elected or appointed volunteer staff members. These staff members recruit others and form a Unit.

The Operational Structure must do two things. One, it must help the congregation avoid a "silo mentality." A silo mentality looks something like this. A congregation establishes strategic goals around Outreach, Nurture and Service. Then, when it comes to the Outreach goal, the members of the Church Council look at the Board of Outreach or Evangelism and say, "Take it." They look at the Nurture goal and say to the Board of Education, "It's all yours." And the same thing happens with the Service goal. They look at the Board of Social Ministry and say, "Take it." So the responsibility of ensuring that the congregation accomplishes its Strategic Goals falls to only three Boards. Meanwhile, the other programmatic Boards spend their time and the congregation's resources doing whatever it is they think their Boards should do. This leads to Boards building silos inside which they work. This silo mentality by the Church Council says, "This is your responsibility, get it done." And the Units get to a point where they say, "This is our responsibility. Do not cross into our territory."

If the units of the Operational Structure are not going to invest congregational resources in accomplishing the goals, why should they have resources to spend on things that the congregational leadership has not deemed strategic? Every unit must determine ways to make contributions to every goal of the congregation. As a result, all of the resources of the congregation will be used to bring about the preferred futures described in the "Corporate" goals. We refer to Strategic Goals as "Corporate" Goals, not because they have anything to do with business, but because they belong to the whole, the "corpus," the entire body of the congregation.

The Operational Structure must make it easy for the Senior Pastor to manage the day-to-day ministry efforts of the congregation. This requires clear lines of authority and accountability. When the Senior Pastor is empowered to select those who will be responsible for various areas of congregational ministry and is allowed to have those people accountable to him/her, it is possible for the Senior Pastor to make certain the resources of the congregation are indeed being used to move the congregation along in its Strategic Direction.

Variations in Operational Structure
The size of congregations and their professional staffs may call for variations in the ways operations are structured. For instance, in a congregation with a small professional staff, it may be necessary for the Senior Pastor to establish a Council of Ministries. This looks similar to a Church Council, but it has two significant differences: 1) The Senior Pastor chairs the Council of Ministries;

and 2) the members of this Council who are the heads of the pro-grammatic ministry Units are accountable to the Senior Pastor for developing, implementing and achieving operational goals.

This Council of Ministries works under the leadership of and in partnership with the Senior Pastor to design and implement the annual ministry plan. The Council of Ministries may be comprised of lay ministers (volunteer staff) and/or professional (paid staff). These lay ministers may be appointed by the Senior Pastor or by the Governance Board, depending on the way the congregation is structured. The structures may vary slightly, but in some way they cover the main areas of church ministry: Education, Outreach, Youth, Spiritual Care and Fellowship.

We believe there should only be one Board that holds the fiduciary role for the congregation. A word concerning elders/deacons and their responsibilities within this new structure might be helpful. In many congregations elders/deacons comprise an additional governance board, supervising the pastor and setting policy for the congregation. In our preferred structure, the elders/deacons, as an extension of the office of the Senior Pastor, are recruited, trained and supervised by the Senior Pastor. They are a part of the operational body and are under the guidance of the Senior Pastor. Their task is to care for the spiritual wellness of the congregation, coordinate worship, serve as a grievance committee and undertake any number of other activities for the congregation and staff.

The benefit of this model is that flexibility is given to the Senior Pastor and staff (paid and/or volunteer) so they can carry out ministry in the most effective and efficient way, while main-taining strong accountability to the Governance Board. With this benefit comes the challenge of maintaining a relationship between the elected ministers and the ordained and professional ministers. This model requires a healthy tension of leadership and supervi-sion between the Board and the Senior Pastor, which translates to a healthy tension between Governance and Operations. And, of course, Governance and Operations are both essential for a solid missional structure. The Governance policies are dynamic with responsibility, authority and accountability clearly defined, consequently guiding this partnership in Christ.

For which of you, intending to build a tower, does not first sit down and estimate the cost, to see whether he has enough to complete it? Otherwise, when he has laid a foundation and is not able to finish, all who see it will begin to ridicule him, saying, "This fellow began to build and was not able to finish."

Luke 14:28-30 (NRSV)

.

Chapter 9

Getting Under Way

*Every day you may make
progress. Every step may be
fruitful. Yet there will stretch out
before you an ever-lengthening,
ever-ascending, ever-improving
path. You know you will never
get to the end of the journey. But
this, so far from discouraging,
only adds to the joy and glory of
the climb.*

Winston Churchill

An important quality of leadership is the ability to bring projects to completion. Restructuring your congregation for mission will require competent, consistent and committed leadership and management. There is no quick fix process that will be effective and ultimately efficient. The transition to a new structure will require focus and patience for the long haul. The following is an outline of the critical and sequential phases of a structural change.

Let's first discuss things you should NOT do.

1. Do not start with a revision of the constitution and by-laws. Eventually you may need to do this; however, it will be more efficient to wait and decide what actually needs revision and what is already in harmony with the new structure. The congregation will need to have clear and persuasive reasons for changing these important articles. The leadership will be better able to discuss the real need after they have studied and written governance policies. The current constitution and by-laws should remain the authoritative documents until you are fully prepared to operate under revisions. This is not the advice of most consultants; however, we believe you will be better served by using the experience and wisdom of congregational leadership to define how things should work (establishing policies) before doing a rewrite of constitution and by-laws.

2. Do not simply use a Board Governance manual copied from another congregation. While it may save some time initially, the lack of participation and ownership will keep you from behaving in new, more productive ways.

3. Do not give the primary study, dialog or decisions regarding structure to any subcommittee, staff or individuals, regardless of how respected and competent they are. Governance belongs to the senior leadership group (Church Council, Vestry or Board of Directors) and they should wrestle with and determine any changes in structure. Eventually a small group will need to write the first draft of the governance manual; however, it should solicit Board input and have a willingness to pursue the new structure.

4. Do not wait until the end of the revisions to inform the congregation about the process and progress of structural revitalization.

5. Do not move forward unless the current Senior Pastor understands the necessary changes for his/her role and is willing to engage in the leadership development necessary to implement the new structure.

6. Do not assume that you should wait to bring a new Pastor on board before you go to Aligned Governance and Operation. If you want this sort of leadership, it should be a part of the interview process.

7. Do not evaluate the success of the change too soon. The systemic nature of a structural renewal will require long-term commitment to implementation and refinement. While initial steps may be successful, greater challenges will happen in the second and third years.

PROCESS FOR IMPLEMENTATION

As congregational leadership considers the restructuring and implementation of Aligned Governance and Operation, there are a number of planning phases to complete and many steps to be taken.

This would be the best time to bring in a consultant to help you explore your options.

PHASE 1   RESEARCH

 Goal

The leadership is well-informed regarding alternative congregational structures and the strengths and weaknesses of their current structure.

 Key Question

Are we structured for effective and efficient mission as best we can be? What is the level of awareness of and/or dissatisfaction with the current structure?

 Process

1. Analysis of current structure for strengths and weaknesses
2. Review of literature regarding congregational structures
3. Survey of leaders and managers in the congregation
4. Exploration and full discussion of structural options
5. Publication of key findings to the congregation

 Decision Point

The senior leadership group must decide if a change in congregational structure would be beneficial. If yes, move to the next phase. If no, utilize the learning from Phase 1 to make minor adjustments and adaptations to the current structure.

PHASE 2   LEADERSHIP AND RESOURCES

 Goal

The leadership will decide if they have the necessary current or future skills and resources to make a structural change.

 Key Question

Do we currently have the leadership necessary to accomplish this change? If not, do we have a reasonable plan for recruiting and utilizing new leadership? Does Aligned Governance and Operations offer the potential for the preferred future in this congregation?

PHASE 2   LEADERSHIP AND RESOURCES

Process

1. Conduct a dialog with the Senior Pastor regarding his/her awareness and self-determination for a structural change.
2. Conduct a full dialog with the current senior leadership group regarding preferred structures.
   a. The senior leadership group determines if the Senior Pastor is willing and capable of filling the new role requirements.
   b. The senior leadership group determines if the congregation has the necessary leaders to fulfill the new requirements.
   c. In an open dialog the senior leadership group determines their readiness for a change.
3. The senior leadership group decides whether to move forward with the structural revision.
4. The senior leadership group publicizes the key decisions to the congregation.

Decision Point

The senior leadership group must decide if a change in congregational structure would be beneficial. If yes, move to the next phase. If no, utilize the learning from Phases 1 and 2 to make minor adjustments and adaptations to the current structure.

PHASE 3   GOVERNANCE MANUAL

Goal

The leadership will draft an initial Governance Manual (see Chapter 10).

Key Question

What policies will give us clear descriptions of the Strategic Direction, Self Discipline, Senior Pastor Parameters and Board and Senior Pastor Partnership?

PHASE 3   GOVERNANCE MANUAL

 Process

1. In full session the senior leadership group brainstorms areas where policies are needed. (See chapter 10 for more details.)

2. If you do not have a relevant Strategic Direction, give significant time in the leadership group (retreat or special meetings) to the development of the Core Values, Mission, Vision, Critical Targets and Corporate Goals. This is not the work of a subcommittee.

3. A subcommittee of three or four people, including the Senior Pastor, should write policies for each policy area.

4. The subcommittee presents the Governance Manual draft to the senior leadership group.

5. The senior leadership group studies the draft and has a dialog regarding their ability to govern with a policy approach.

6. If the senior leadership group determines revisions need to be made to the manual, the drafting committee will make these revisions and bring the revised manual back to the senior leadership group.

7. The senior leadership group adopts the manual, recognizing that it is a dynamic document and will require ongoing revision and refinement. The manual is always a work in progress.

8. The senior leadership group informs the congregation of their progress.

 Decision Point

The senior leadership group must decide if Aligned Governance and Operations would be beneficial. If yes, move to the next phase. If no, utilize the learning from Phase 1-3 to make adjustments to the current structure.

PHASE 4   CONSTITUTION AND BY-LAWS

 Goal

The leadership will present revisions to the constitution and by-laws that are in harmony with the new structure.

PHASE 4   CONSTITUTION AND BY-LAWS

Key Question

Can we simply make minor revisions to our current constitution and by-laws, or do we need to develop new documents?

Process

1. Appoint a constitutional revision committee of people who fully understand the proposed structural change. Ask the committee to review the current governance documents and to determine what needs revision, adaptation or new language.

2. Ask the committee to harmonize these articles of incorporation with the new structure.

3. Introduce the revisions to the leadership group for adoption in preparation for a presentation to the congregation.

PHASE 5   CONGREGATIONAL AWARENESS

Goal

The congregation is well-informed concerning the complete process and results of the leadership's thinking. The leadership demonstrates appreciation for and patience with resistance to change.

Key Question

Have we fully engaged the congregation in dialog regarding the current structure's strengths and weaknesses? Have we made a convincing case for change to the structure of our congregation?

The more you work with the governance manual, the smarter you will be about governance. The smarter you are about governance, the better you will refine your manual.

PHASE 5   CONGREGATIONAL AWARENESS

Process

1. Design, promote and conduct two to three congregational meetings which include a presentation and open forum.

   Presentation:
   - Describe the process of study and decision.
   - Describe the perceived strengths and weaknesses of the current structure and the strengths and weaknesses of the proposed structure.
   - Describe what changes should be accomplished and when.
   - Have a printed handout listing the points of revision needed in the constitution and by-laws.

   Forum Exchange:
   - If the group is small, respond to everyone's observations and questions.
   - Record every comment.
   - If the group is large, break into small groups and ask a recorder/reporter in each group to collect the observations and questions of his/her group.
   - The leadership should listen carefully and explain the model rather than defend it.

2. Publish the presentation and a summary of the members' comments from the forums and distribute them to all voting members.

3. Based on the feedback of the congregation, the leadership group determines whether to move forward. It may be that some adjustments to the revisions of the constitution and by-laws will be necessary before you can move forward.

PHASE 5   CONGREGATIONAL AWARENESS

Decision Point

The senior leadership group must decide if they believe the congregation will adopt the proposed constitution and/or by-laws. If yes, move to the next phase. If no, determine what changes would be necessary for adoption by the congregation. If the senior leadership group is convinced no adoption is possible, utilize the learning from Phases 1-5 to make adjustments to the current structure.

PHASE 6   CONGREGATIONAL ADOPTION

Goal

The congregation embraces the proposed structural revision and is prepared to participate in the implementation.

Key Question

What is the proper constitutional procedure necessary to amend the constitution and by-laws?

Process

1. Presentation to Congregation
    a. Change the by-laws and constitution according to the established procedures.
        i.   Adoption by the congregation
        ii. Establishment of a time frame for implementation
        iii. Development of a strategy for transition
    b. Conclude with an up or down vote on the constitutional and/or by-law changes (usually two-thirds majority required).
2. Election of New Board

Decision Point

If the congregation adopts the amendments, the senior leadership group must insure the election of the new board and move to the next phase. Should the congregation vote no, the senior leadership group determines if the congregation's opposition is caused by 1) their belief that it is simply not the right structure or 2) a lack of understanding. If (2) is true, it may be that future communication and study is needed. If (1) is true, the senior leadership group should implement the learning and awareness gained and keep working toward the mission.

PHASE 7   IMPLEMENTATION

 Goal
The Board will successfully initiate the new structure for governance and the Senior Pastor will successfully initiate a new operational structure and plan.

 Key Question
What must the Board and the Senior Pastor do to initiate a successful genesis of the newly adopted structure?

 Process

1. Orientation of New Board to Aligned Organizational Governance
   a. Faith exploration
   b. Community building
   c. New Board is taken through the governance manual with discussions of how it goes about its work (Special attention to Board and member responsibilities)
   d. Board is helped to explore what its meetings might include
   e. Vision casting and dialog
2. Operational Structure
   a. Design by Senior Pastor with Staff counsel
   b. Strategy for implementation
   c. Time frame
   d. New responsibilities
   e. Accountability System
   f. Thanksgiving for and honoring of past servants
   g. Recruitment of a new team
3. Operational Path (means) aligned with the Strategic Direction (ends)

PHASE 7   IMPLEMENTATION

 Process

4. Re-charter of every Operational Unit
   a. Establish the purpose and objectives of the Unit. (Their purpose is to accomplish the mission of the congregation through their particular focus or ministry effort.)
   b. Establish the authority of the Unit. Are they to study, recommend, decide and/or implement?
   c. Establish to which staff member the unit reports.
   d. Establish measurable goals, objectives and action plans.
   e. Establish a process for evaluation including who, how and when.
   f. Establish a clear time frame, indicating the beginning and the end.

PHASE 8   CONTINUAL STRUCTURAL DEVELOPMENT

 Goal

Continual renewal of the governance and operational structure that will be effective and efficient for accomplishing the mission.

 Key Question

How will the Governance Board and Senior Pastor continue to effectively represent the Stewards of the congregation, providing a relevant and sustainable mission?

PHASE 8 CONTINUAL STRUCTURAL DEVELOPMENT

 Process

1. The Board ensures Self Discipline policies that specify self evaluation.
   a. At every meeting
   b. Of fellow Board members
   c. In more detail quarterly
      • Review Strategic Direction policies
      • Review Board Self Discipline policies
      • Review Senior Pastor Parameters policies
      • Review Board and Senior Pastor Partnership policies
2. The Senior Pastor ensures an Operational Path in alignment with the policies of the congregation.
   a. Supervision
   b. Accountability
   c. Formal and informal evaluation of staff and the Senior Pastor

This chapter was an overview of the implementation process. Whether you are a small congregation, a large congregation or even a new mission start, the dynamics of a missional structure (see page 19) are impacting your congregation. But one approach does not apply to all. How these dynamics play out will be different for each congregation, and each congregation will need to design a process that fits its reality.

*For the kingdom of God depends
not on talk but on power.*

1 Corinthians 4:20 (NRSV)

Chapter 10
Developing the Governance Manual

But peace does not rest in the
charters and covenants alone. It
lies in the hearts and minds of
all people. So let us not rest all
our hopes on parchment and on
paper, let us strive to build peace,
a desire for peace, a willingness to
work for peace in the hearts and
minds of all of our people.

John F. Kennedy

Aligned Governance and Operations requires a dynamic and comprehensive Governance Manual. The development of the manual requires extensive Board dialog and careful writing and publishing of the Board's decisions. If that sounds like a lot of work, it is. There is no shortcut to Aligned Governance. During this extensive process, the leadership is developing a greater focus and the ability to function as a governing Board.

You can use this chapter to develop the Governance Manual that will best fit your congregation. The Governance Manual, unlike your constitution and by-laws, is flexible and versatile. It should be with you at every Board meeting and serve as the framework for your leadership as a Board.

Board Self Discipline requires the ongoing review and revision of all policy. As a working document, the Governance Manual is adopted with the understanding that it is, and will continue to be, a work in progress. Boards will not be compliant with all the new policies overnight. You will embrace the concept and continue to develop the specifics. It will be necessary for the Board, over a long period of time, to implement all of the procedures and documentation that the manual has established, including elections, self evaluation, a means of monitoring, etc.

The real benefit of Aligned Governance is systemic. The work of the Governance Board will become more focused. The time required to decide and implement should decrease. Over time, the policies will become a corporate memory that guides the Board on to more Strategic Direction with less reactionary management. Most importantly, when you codify your dialog into policy, you leave a legacy of leadership to future Boards.

The parameter of authority and responsibility should be articulated in the constitution and by-laws established by the congregation and should never be altered by any one person or subgroup; the decision must be congregational. Policies of governance should be established by the Board because the Board has been charged with giving leadership to the congregation. Policies should never violate the constitution or by-laws.

Board Basics: The Governance Manual

A Board governs with one voice using policies in four primary areas of responsibility: Strategic Direction, Board Self Discipline, Senior Pastor Parameters and Board and Senior Pastor Partnership. In order to fulfill the requirements of those who are the stewards of its ministry, the policies must be proactive and provide leadership for the church. The Christian steward should always be asking how to make an impact on the served in the name of Christ.

The following outline includes questions that help guide you through the development of a Governance Manual. Examples are given to provide a format for the policies. The previous chapter offered recommendations for how to use the questions and examples that follow (Phase 3 of Chapter 9).

STRATEGIC DIRECTION

Core Values

What are the deep-seated, defining convictions held by the congregation that cause certain outcomes to be preferred over opposite or converse outcomes? Congregations may have as few as five or as many as eight Core Values.

Mission

How would you clearly and concisely state (in 25 words or less) the unique reasons or purpose for the existence and efforts of your congregation? Congregations often have similar Mission Statements because they share a similar commission from our Lord Jesus.

Vision

What snapshot of the future in the hearts and minds of the leaders will simply not fade away? A Vision is more than a slogan. It captures the next phase of development for the congregation responding to the guidance of the Holy Spirit. The Mission Vision should fit your congregation in your community in the location and time frame God has given you. It can be two sentences or two paragraphs.

Critical Targets

On what special foci of work (groups of people or areas of effort) must the congregation make significant impact in order to effectively honor its Core Values and pursue its Mission? Selection of Critical Targets is highly influenced by the Vision.

Sample Policy

Utilizing diverse styles to communicate God's all-powerful grace, Gospel-focused worship engages new worshippers in language they understand and inspires those who are rooted in the heritage.

Corporate Goals

How is each Critical Target being met? What is the preferred future condition of the each target? The Corporate Goal describes how the target is contributing to an effective pursuit of the mission. There should be one Corporate Goal for each Critical Target.

Sample Policy

Gospel-focused worship is an uplifting experience that addresses the issues people face on a day to day basis. It engages new worshippers in language they understand as well as inspires those who are rooted in the heritage of the faith. Using a diversity of styles, it communicates God's all-powerful grace to more and more people in an excellent and passionate manner.

Indicators of Success

What three to four indicators best describe success for each Corporate Goal? These are not hard-line goals, but are a starting point where all conversation about progress begins.

Stewards

Who are the Stewards of the ministry of Christ in the congregation? How would you describe them? What efforts will be made to listen to the Stewards and to communicate with them? Are all members Stewards? Are there people who regularly participate in and benefit from the ministry of your congregation but are not Stewards?

Sample Policy

The main responsibility of the Governance Board is to represent the Stewards of the congregation. Stewards are those who are the Body of Christ in this place and who, in faith, consciously invest themselves and their resources in order to enhance and expand the spreading of the Gospel through the congregation's mission and ministry. The Board recognizes no individual or group as the sole steward of the congregation.

The Served

Whom does the congregation serve? How would you describe them? Certainly, Stewards are being served, but are there not others the congregation should be serving as well? How are the Served to be treated by the congregation?

Sample Policies

- The Served are those who utilize and benefit from the ministries offered by the congregation to honor its Core Values and pursue its Mission.
- The congregation shall offer the highest quality ministries with honesty, integrity and sensitivity to the Served.

The Cost to the Communities of the Congregation

What will it cost the congregation to honor its Core Values, pursue its Mission and accomplish its Strategic Direction? While it will not be possible to detail the exact costs, there is a way to describe what you want to happen.

Sample Policy
Biblical stewardship shall be utilized to guarantee that ministries to achieve the Strategic Direction shall be offered at a fair and improving cost to the congregation's communities. Costs for such ministries shall not infringe upon the congregation's capability to accomplish the Strategic Direction.

Strategic Alliances
Is the congregation in this alone, or are there other individuals and organizations who could serve as allies? Strategic Alliances are mutually beneficial relationships with other organizations or individuals. These alliances are built upon a common vision or goal which allows all parties to honor their Core Values, enhance the pursuit of their mission and maintain operational autonomy. Does (should) your congregation have such relationships?

BOARD SELF DISCIPLINE

Board Responsibilities
What are the overall responsibilities of the Governance Board when it comes to the congregation? What should the Governance Board do to carry out its constitutional responsibilities in the manner it feels will be most effective?

Sample Policy
The overall responsibility of the Board is to provide a powerful, ethical, responsible and spiritual pursuit of the congregation's mission. To that end, the Board shall:

Sample Policy (continued)

- Make certain the Strategic Direction (Core Values, Mission, Vision, Critical Targets and Corporate Goals) of the congregation is the driving force for all activities and related ministries.

- Provide oversight of all congregational activities by establishing and monitoring appropriateness of and adherence to policies that guide the efforts of the Senior Pastor. Ensure that the policy and financial decisions are executed in accordance with the constitution and by-laws of the congregation.

- Communicate regularly to the Stewards the pertinent activities of the Board and remain open to communication from the Stewards.

- Exercise particular concern for the spiritual and physical welfare of the Senior Pastor.

Membership Responsibilities

What are the Board members' responsibilities to each other? How will they conduct themselves as Board members? What will they do to continue the development of their faith lives? What will they do to be ready for Board meetings? How will they treat each other and the Senior Pastor? Will they speak with one voice? What about "conflict of interest" situations? Are they expected to serve in other aspects of the ministry of the congregation? How do they handle it when they perceive something is not right? What discipline process will they use to make sure they are living up to their responsibilities?

Enunciating Governing Policies

What kind of policies will the Board write in order to govern by policy?

Philosophy of Governance

To what philosophical approach will the Board adhere in its governance efforts? Should the Board ever surrender the judgment of the whole Board to the expertise of one or two individuals? What authority should a Governance Board never assume? How does a Board carry out its financial responsibilities? Do Board members have any authority outside of the Board meeting? How does the Board go about developing governance policies and then ensuring they are followed?

Calling/Hiring of the Senior Pastor

What responsibilities does the Governance Board have in the calling/hiring of a Senior Pastor? What steps should it go through?

Calling/Hiring of Other Workers

What responsibilities does the Governance Board have in the calling/hiring of other staff? What steps should it go through? What role does the Senior Pastor have in the calling/hiring of other staff?

Election of Governance Board Members

While much of this will be in the constitution and by-laws, the procedures should be clearly restated and further enhanced in the Governance Manual. What responsibilities does the Governance Board have to the congregation in the process of electing Board members? What does the nominating process look like? How are congregational members informed of their rights in this process? What are the qualifications for membership on the Board? Are there any restrictions to membership on the Board? (For example, can the spouse of a staff person serve on the Board? Can two brothers or a mother and son serve on the Board at the same time?) What are the term limits? How are vacancies filled?

Sample Policies

Vacancies:

- Vacancies that occur on the Governance Board shall be filled in accordance with applicable provisions of the by-laws. However, only individuals deemed qualified by the Nominating Committee may be appointed to fill a vacancy.

- An appointment to fill a vacancy on the Board shall always be to complete an unexpired term and in no case shall such an appointment work in contradiction to the election of approximately one-third of the Board each year.

- Every effort shall be made to fill vacancies within three months of their occurrence; however, if there is less than one year of service left in the term, the position may remain vacant until it is filled through the election process.

Board Training and Self-Review

What training comes with the Board experience and how often is the training offered in order for the individual members to become more adept at the governing process? How often will the Board evaluate its own effectiveness and how will it do so?

Officers of the Board

How many officers will the Board have? How are they elected? What are their responsibilities? Some of these questions will be answered in the constitution and by-laws, but they should appear in the manual in detail.

Sample Policies

The Secretary shall:

- Serve on the Executive Committee of the Board.
- Maintain the minutes of all meetings of the Governance Board and Congregational Assembly and ensure that copies of all such minutes are kept on file in the church office.
- Conduct all official correspondence of the Governance Board and the Congregational Assembly.
- Be thoroughly familiar with the congregation's constitution and by-laws and serve as the primary resource to the Board and Congregational Assembly for questions concerning the same.

Committees of the Board

Will the Board have committees? If so, how many and what will be their responsibilities? How are committees chartered, and how do they go about their work?

Executive Committee of the Board

Is there an Executive Committee of the Board? What is its authority and what are its duties? Many constitutions and by-laws mandate an Executive Committee and its membership, but this decision should be left to the Governance Board as it evaluates its needs for effective governance. What are the limitations to the authority of the Executive Committee?

Responsibilities to the Stewards of the Congregation

What are the responsibilities of the Governance Board to the Stewards? Beyond the obvious members, who are Stewards? Are there other people who have felt stewardship responsibility for the ministry of Christ in this place and at this time? How often should the Governance Board report to the Stewards and in what manner?

Dialog with Stewards

Does the Board have a clear picture of who the Stewards are? How will the Board solicit input from them? What is the responsibility of the Board with regard to the Stewards? Remember, the main responsibility of the Governance Board is to represent the Stewards of the congregation.

Board Calendar, Agenda and Meeting Structure

Does the Board have a well-developed sequence for its annual responsibilities? Some things have to be done in certain months; others have more flexibility. Does the Board have an agenda it follows regularly for consistency in going about its work? How does the Board handle guests at its meetings?

SENIOR PASTOR PARAMETERS

Writing parameters for the operations led by the Senior Pastor often proves to be a difficult task for Boards. The recommendation here is that you identify the areas in which you have concerns and then write limiting statements. You write the parameters in the negative. "The Senior pastor will not..." or "The Senior Pastor will not fail to..." This activity is often resisted by Boards. They ask, "Why does everything have to be so negative?" It is not intended to be negative. This section, unlike the Strategic Direction where you state what should be accomplished, states what should not be done as the Senior Pastor and staff strive to pursue the Strategic Direction.

If you were to define everything a Senior Pastor should do, it would be a very long list. The list of parameters is more finite and can be covered in a few pages. This also assures the congregation that the Board has specifically set expectations and boundaries for the Senior Pastor's actions. Unfortunately, some congregations have gone through the difficult task of establishing boundaries after some sort of unacceptable conduct has occurred. We strongly recommend avoiding a minimalist approach to establishing governing policies.

When you talk to those who have worked with this over a period of time, you will find out that it is actually a liberating way to deal with the Senior Pastor. Basically, the Board is saying to the Senior Pastor, "You know from the Strategic Direction what we want to accomplish as a congregation. Do whatever is necessary; just do not cross these lines. You do not have to come back for permission as long as you conduct ministry within these parameters." Any other approach means that the Senior Pastor should always come back for permission.

Primary Parameter

If you had to write one statement to cover all the things you did not want the Senior Pastor to do, how would you word it?

Sample Policy

While representing the Congregation, the Senior Pastor shall not act in a manner that is unethical, imprudent, illegal or inconsistent with the constitution, by-laws and governance polices of the congregation.

Communication with and Support of the Board

As the senior staff person for the Governance Board, how would you describe in broad strokes what you want the Senior Pastor to do for the Board?

Sample Policies

- The Senior Pastor shall not permit the Board to be uninformed or unsupported in its work.

Sample Policies (continued)

- The Senior Pastor shall not allow the Board to be unaware of:
    1. Relevant trends that impact the ministry of the congregation.
    2. Anticipated adverse media coverage.
    3. Crises affecting the work, health or safety of staff.
    4. Judicatory [Synod, District, Presbytery, Archdiocese] directions and recommendations.
- The Senior Pastor shall not fail to provide the Board with information and ideas the Board needs to make informed decisions.

Financial

What do you want the Senior Pastor to avoid doing when he/she is overseeing the day-to-day finances of the congregation? Would you prefer that annual financial plans not be adopted after the start of the fiscal year? Would you prefer that he/she not plan to expend more funds than are reasonably expected to be received in any fiscal year? Do you want to avoid an unsound financial condition that could jeopardize the achievement of the Strategic Direction? How would you describe an unsound financial condition in your congregation? What is the monetary amount your Senior Pastor may borrow for working capital without the permission of the Governance Board? What amount of time is too long for short term debt? Do you want the Senior Pastor to put limits on how cash and checks are handled in the congregation?

Asset Protection

What are the minimum and maximum amounts you want the Senior Pastor to ensure against theft and casualty losses? Do you want to set limits on the use of your plant, grounds and equipment?

How do you tell the Pastor that he/she may not fail to protect intellectual property of the congregation? Can the Senior Pastor purchase items over a pre-established amount without comparative bids?

Operational Structure

What parameters do you want to put on the operational structure established by the Senior Pastor? Would it be acceptable for the Senior Pastor to allow a staff person to continue a favorite ministry in the congregation which contributes nothing to the Strategic Direction? Do you want the Senior Pastor to be able to operate without a short-term succession plan in the case of his/her prolonged absence, short of a disability?

Operational Crisis Management Plan

Should the Senior Pastor allow the congregation to function without an Operational Crisis Management Plan?

Personnel

Do you want the Senior Pastor to operate without clearly defined Operational Policies which contain personnel policies and other operational procedural guidelines?

Sample Policies

- The Senior Pastor shall not allow the congregation to operate without effective, established operational policies which, with regard to personnel, clarify personnel rules, provide for effective handling of grievances, provide for evaluation procedures and protect against wrongful conditions, such as nepotism and preferential treatment for personal reasons.

Sample Policies (continued)

- The Senior Pastor shall not promise or imply permanent or guaranteed employment.

- The Senior Pastor shall not allow positions to exist where adequate resources are not available for a qualified person, who has been assigned to the position, to succeed.

- The Senior Pastor shall not fail to conduct annual written staff performance appraisals and to share the results with the appropriate staff member.

- The Senior Pastor shall not fail to have a pre-determined approach (such as Aligned Organizational Operations) to his/her supervision of the staff.

Compensation

What are the Senior Pastor's Parameters when it comes to compensation? Must compensation fall within the ranges identified in the Operations Manual? Can the compensation deviate materially from the geographic or professional market skills of the workers? Can the Senior Pastor allow salary increases to be based on anything other than merit?

Long Range Outlook

What would you do should the Senior Pastor ever fail to provide to the Governance Board an annual long range outlook? Should that outlook be based on the Strategic Direction of the congregation?

Planning

When the Senior Pastor leads the staff through the development of an Operational Path for the ministry of the congregation, are there any parameters? Must the Operational Path be built on the Strategic Direction? Can the annual financial plan be developed without due consideration to an Operational Path that has been developed with the express purpose of moving the congregation along the path of its Strategic Direction?

Ministry Programs

Is it all right for the Senior Pastor to allow ministry programs and services that do not contribute to the accomplishment of the congregation's Strategic Direction as established by the Board? Is it all right for the Staff to "operate" their areas of ministry without advice and counsel from members of the congregation? Is it acceptable for staff to go about their ministries without an intentionally developed, well-defined, individual, operational path? Do you want staff to be "Lone Rangers" or do you want staff to train others for ministry within their area of responsibility? Does the Governance Board want to hear only from the Senior Pastor when it comes to operational reports, or do they, from time to time, want to hear from other operational staff?

Sample Policies

- The Senior Pastor shall not allow full time staff to conduct their ministries without a commitment to the "priesthood of all believers" and thus, a commitment to the training and utilization of lay members of the congregation in their respective ministry areas.

- The Senior Pastor shall not fail to have the Senior Staff engage with the Board in conversation and edification at least once a year.

Strategic Alliances

Does the Board want the Senior Pastor to pursue appropriate strategic alliances? Alliances might include neighborhood organizations, social services agencies or other churches working toward a shared mission.

Gifts and Bequests

Does the Board expect the Senior Pastor to ensure there is a plan to promote and receive gifts and bequests for the congregation? What parameters are to be placed on such practices? Can the Senior Pastor accept gifts that are not fully aligned with the Strategic Direction? Or gifts that are too restrictive in their use?

BOARD AND SENIOR PASTOR PARTNERSHIP

Actions Requiring Board Approval

Which decisions must always be determined by the Board and never delegated to others? (For example, the election of its officers if so stated in the by-laws, the selection of the auditor and receipt of the financial audit or the appointment of legal counsel) Which decisions must remain with the assembly of members and never be delegated to the Governance Board (For example, the hiring or calling of the Senior Pastor, the incurring of long-term debt, the dissolution or merger of the congregation, or the election or removal of a member of the Governance Board)?

Manner of Delegating

Is it clear that the responsibility of the Governance Board is to develop, monitor and enforce governing policy, not implement it? Does the Governance Board ever delegate authority to anyone other than the Senior Pastor? If so, under what circumstances? What sort of contact should the members of the Governance Board have with staff outside of the Board meetings? How detailed is the Board going to be in determining appropriate actions by the staff?

Sample Policies

- The Board shall address only broad levels of issues in policies leaving lesser levels, such as operational policies, to the discretion of the Senior Pastor.

- The authority of the Senior Pastor shall begin where the specific responsibilities of the Board end. Except as required by governing policies or law, decisions of the Senior Pastor do not need approval by the Board.

Senior Pastor Function

What is the Senior Pastor empowered to do within the congregation? How much permission must he/she pursue in carrying out his/her responsibility to lead the congregation toward the Strategic Direction?

Senior Pastor Accountability

For what is the Senior Pastor responsible and to whom is the Senior Pastor accountable? What constitutes acceptable performance on the part of the Senior Pastor?

Exceeding Senior Pastor Parameters

What are the procedures when an Senior Pastor Parameter is violated? Who is responsible for calling attention to the matter? What steps are to be taken and by whom? How is the action of the staff brought back into alignment with the exceeded Parameter? What happens if the Parameter is crossed again? What if a staff member believes that a Parameter has been violated, but the Senior Pastor does not?

Means of Monitoring

How does the Governance Board ensure that it is receiving the information it needs in order to carry out its leadership responsibilities? What reports does it want from the Senior Pastor, and how often should these reports be generated? What options does the Board have if it senses that it is not receiving full or accurate information? What standard is used to determine compliance with the Board's mandates for reporting information?

Other Policies

What other policies does the Governance Board believe are necessary? The Governance Board can adopt any policies it believes are essential to good governance. The Congregation has elected the Board to govern all aspects of Congregational life.

Every agenda item should go through a simple Aligned Organizational Governance routine.

1. Do we have a policy that deals with this issue?

2. If not, what policy should we establish?

3. If we do, is it clear enough to act on or rule on with regard to this issue? Or, if not, should we revise the policy to make it more comprehensive?

Other Resources

Some congregations have simply copied a Governance Manual from another congregation. This is not recommended. Anyone who has gone through a thorough implementation approach will tell you the process is worth as much as the product.

Frequently congregations seek outside help. This requires a consultant or judicatory facilitator who:

- Understands the philosophy of Aligned Organizational Governance and Operations as well as the process.

- Has a proven methodology for moving the congregation through the process.

- Can coach the Board Chair and assist the Board in learning the "ins and outs" of Aligned Governance and Operations.

- Can coach the Senior Pastor to understand his/her role and the implications for his/her ministry and can work with the staff in the same manner.

A Dynamic Document

The creation of the policy manual requires significant effort from the board. It is a valuable investment for the sake of your congregation. You can't have a new aligned governance structure without this pivotal document. After you have completed the document you can enjoy the benefit of your work for years to come. This does not mean, however, you are finished with the manual. The manual will be used in every meeting by every member.

The continuing additions, refinements and clarifications will be an ongoing process. Updated copies should be provided regularly.

The plans of the mind belong to mortals, but the answer of the tongue is from the LORD. All one's ways may be pure in one's own eyes, but the LORD weighs the spirit. Commit your work to the LORD, and your plans will be established.

Proverbs 16:1-3 (NRSV)

Epilogue

Joseph's Bones

We believe that aligned governance in your congregation not only contributes to effective and efficient structure, it provides a legacy of leadership extended to the stewards that follow. A dynamic governance manual for your congregation is like Joseph's bones for the children of Israel. When Pharaoh let the people go, Moses took with him the bones of Joseph. He was fulfilling a solemn oath the Israelites had made to Joseph. We can imagine that as they journeyed through the wilderness for 40 years, Joseph's bones provided a powerful connection to their history and a purpose for their future.

The slaves of Egypt would have to establish a new culture. God was using the transition in the wilderness to accomplish his transformation of a new nation. (Ex. 13:17-19) If your manual is developed through prayerful insight and deliberation, the policies become a gift to all the stewards who follow.

In North America the post-modern, post-Christian culture is a reality. The impact of this cultural climate has had a dramatic effect on the church. As a Spirit-led steward you are living your mission as the body of Christ in this changing culture. You are forced to rethink and restructure the way you accomplish the mission. However, the mission remains the same.

As a Spirit-led Steward, you know the victory has already been accomplished through Jesus Christ. You consider it a privilege to be a part of His eternal plan. Instead of reacting to the culture, you, by God's grace, are transforming the culture. This is the legacy of God's people since the beginning of time.

Therefore, since we are surrounded by so great a cloud of witnesses, let us also lay aside every weight and the sin that clings so closely, and let us run with perseverance the race that is set before us, looking to Jesus the pioneer and perfecter of our faith, who for the sake of the joy that was set before him endured the cross, disregarding its shame, and has taken his seat at the right hand of the throne of God.

Hebrews 12:1-2 (NRSV)

APPENDIX

An Emergent Theology for Emerging Churches, Ray S. Anderson, Inter Varsity Press, Downers Grove, IL, 2006

The Externally Focused Church, Rick Rusaw and Eric Swanson, Group Publishing, Loveland, CO, 2004

Hit the Bullseye, How Denominations Can Aim Congregations at the Mission Field, Paul Borden, Abingdon Press, Nashville 2003

The Nature of Authentic Christian Leadership, Aubrey Malphurs, Being Leaders, Baker Books, Grand Rapids, MI 2003

Direct Hit, Aiming Real Leaders at the Mission Field, Paul Borden, Abingdon Press, Nashville 2006

Six Marks of Discipleship for a Changing Church, Michael Foss, Power Surge, Augsburg Fortress, Minneapolis 2000

The Present Future, Six Tough Questions for the Church, Reggie McNeal, Jossey-Bass, San Francisco, 2003

Pastor, The Theology and Practice of Ordained Ministry, William Willimon, Abingdon Press, Nashville 2002

Simple Church, Returning to God's Process for Making Disciples, Thom Rainer and Eric Geiger, B and H Publishing Group, Nashville, 2006

Transforming Church, Liberating Structures for Ministry, Robin Greenwood, Society for Promoting Christian Knowledge, Cippenham, Wiltshire, Great Britain, 2002

The Unnecessary Pastor, Rediscovering the Call, Marva Dawn and Eugene Peterson, William Eerdmans Publishing Company, Grand Rapids, MI 2000

Deep Change, Discovering the Leader Within, Robert Quinn, Jossey-Bass, San Francisco, 1996

Books on Structure

Boards That Make a Difference, John Carver, Jossey Bass, San Francisco, 1990

Reinventing Your Board, A Step-by-Step Guide to Implementing Policy Governance, John Carver and Miriam Mayhew Carer, Jossey Bass, San Francisco, 1997

Transforming Church Boards, Charles Olson, The Alban Institute, New York, 1995

Governance as Leadership, Richard Chait, William Ryan and Barbara Taylor, Wiley and Sons, Hoboken, New Jersey 2005

Managing the Non-Profit Organization, Practices and Principles, Peter Drucker, HarperCollins Publishers, New York 1990

Building Effective Boards for Religious Organizations, A Handbook for Trustees, Presidents and Church Leaders, Thomas Holland and David Hester (editors), Jossey-Bass, San Francisco, 2000

CONSULTING AND TRAINING SERVICES

"Excellence of Character and Power to Achieve"

Design and Implementation of a Planning Process

CORNERSTONE works with you to develop a process for closing the gap between your present situation and your desired future.

Team Effectiveness

CORNERSTONE facilitates a process for the transformation of both the tasks and relationships of your working teams.

Meeting Facilitation

CORNERSTONE offers assistance for getting the most out of your meetings.

Board Governance

CORNERSTONE provides consultation services designed to assess, renew and sustain effective governance and operations within your organization.

Leadership Training

CORNERSTONE consultants are also premier trainers and speakers. They manage complex training processes on a variety of topics such as human resource development and organizational effectiveness.

www.CornerstoneFactor.com